Entrance to the Royal Palace, Edinburgh Castle

EDINBURGH
CELEBRITY CITY GUIDE

Joanne Soroka

First published in 2013 by
The Crowood Press Ltd
Ramsbury, Marlborough
Wiltshire SN8 2HR

www.crowood.com

British Library Cataloguing-in-Publication Data
A catalogue record for this book is available from the British Library.

ISBN 978 1 84797 487 7

Graphic design, layout, and maps by Peggy Issenman, www.peggyandco.ca
Printed and bound in India by Replika Press Pvt Ltd

CONTENTS

Edinburgh Castle from the Princes Street Gardens.

PREFACE

Connecting Edinburgh and celebrities might at first seem odd. Don't they all live in Paris, London or New York? The celebrities in this book are, however, people of real accomplishment, many of whom are household names. Edinburgh has been a centre of achievement for centuries. From Bonnie Prince Charlie to Alexander Graham Bell to the Bay City Rollers, they all made an impact. Do you want to know about the real Mrs Doubtfire? Or where Tony Blair planned his campaign for the leadership of the Labour Party? You may even want to find out where fictional characters such as Inspector Rebus go for a quick drink.

Edinburgh has long been a hub of intellectual life, spawning or attracting the most intelligent and determined in the country. In particular, the Scottish Enlightenment of the second half of the eighteenth century was a fertile time for philosophers, artists and writers. This was the time of the rise of the scientific method, increasing secularism and scepticism – questioning which only increased through time. Today Edinburgh is still a centre of learning and innovation, whether in physics or restaurants.

Each celebrity has a page with their image, a short biography and a picture of an object, work of art or building associated with them. Colour-coded maps on pages 114–129 show the places they lived, worked, where the objects can be seen, a grave, a statue, whatever is available to be visited. For the living, current addresses are not included to protect their privacy, and some buildings are now private homes, so please do not disturb current residents. Other buildings have unfortunately been demolished, with the maps marking the approximate site.

The collection of one hundred celebrities is a personal choice, since there could easily have been twice as many. They are divided into six categories: artists, writers, performers, doers, pioneers and the uncategorizable. You can trace their movements around the city, using the grid references and postcodes in the text, together with the maps. You can find out whether a celebrity lived down the road or next door. There are also artefacts available to see, with most of the museums and galleries mentioned having free admission.

Edinburgh does not have the London system of standardized blue plaques indicating the homes of the famous. Plaques of various types have been erected by organizations as diverse as the Japan Sherlock Holmes Club and the International Association for the Study of Pain, but some places have nothing. If you look up to first-floor level, however, you may be rewarded by the sight of one of them or an inscription carved in stone. (North Americans, please remember that in Britain, your first floor is the ground floor, and your second floor is the first floor.)

The guidebook is designed so that you can dip into it, for example if you have a particular interest in Sean Connery or Mary Queen of Scots. Maybe you are curious about all of Edinburgh's many writers. Or you may discover someone you'd never heard of, finding his of her story fascinating. This new type of guidebook will help you to see Edinburgh from the point of view of its most celebrated residents and show you how to walk in their footsteps. And it is best to walk – slowly absorbing the atmosphere, the different eras and generations whose ghosts and living people inhabit the city's streets.

1

ARTISTS

As well as the expected painters, this category is populated with architects, sculptors, photographers, printmakers and those who work in glass and textiles. Architects in particular have shaped the way Edinburgh looks today. James Craig devised the plan for the New Town – new in the eighteenth century, that is – from an idea for a planned suburb. Following him, Robert Adam and William Playfair put their mainly Georgian stamp on Edinburgh, whose Old and New Towns are UNESCO World Heritage Sites. The beautiful buildings and terraces designed by these three architects helped to secure this honour.

Sir Henry Raeburn and John Kay were contemporaries who would have witnessed the building of the New Town, and Raeburn as a property developer contributed to its expansion. However, he is primarily known for his superb portraits of the celebrities of the era, and many of those he depicted are still well-known – Adam Smith, David Hume, James Boswell and others. His portrait of the skating minister has become the emblem of the National Galleries of Scotland. John Kay's caricatures of the same people annoyed some of them to the extent that he was beaten up and (unsuccessfully) prosecuted.

In the Victorian era, David Octavius Hill and Robert Adamson took up the new technology of photography and turned it into an art form. Their short-lived partnership was responsible for numerous portraits of the famous as well as those of modest birth. The Scottish Colourists stuck to painting, but brought a new sensibility to it. Two of its number were Samuel Peploe and Francis Cadell, both of whom wanted to create a Scottish idiom in visual art.

In the later Victorian era, it started to be possible for determined women to become artists. The first professional in Edinburgh was Phoebe Traquair, whose work spanned several fields, from murals to enamels and textiles. She set the scene for twentieth-century women, namely Anne Redpath and later Dame Elizabeth Blackadder. Most recently, Alison Kinnaird combines working with etched glass and playing the Scottish harp.

Sir Eduardo Paolozzi started from humble beginnings but became one of the most prominent British artists of the twentieth century, with his public sculptures in locations around Edinburgh and other cities. The painter John Bellany also rose to fame with pictures of strange combinations of fish and humans, showing his roots in the nearby fishing community of Port Seton.

Edinburgh and its people feature in many of the images created by the artists. And the city itself is a work of art, its Old Town replete with ancient buildings, a castle and palace, and its New Town resplendent with sweeps of Georgian terraces.

Elizabeth Blackadder is known for enjoying drawing her cats. Louis has posed for her here (not on public display).

～ ROBERT ADAM ～

1728–92, ARCHITECT

Robert Adam was born in Kirkcaldy, his family moving that same year to Edinburgh and living in the Canongate. The son of a prominent architect, he was educated at the **Royal High School** *Map p126* **S14** (High School Yards, now Archaeology Building of University of Edinburgh, EH1 1LZ) and the **University of Edinburgh** *Map p126* **R14** (Old College, South Bridge, plaque inside entrance on left, EH8 9YL). His schooling was interrupted by illness and Bonnie Prince Charlie's, q.v., Jacobite Rebellion. He initially wanted to become an artist, but with his elder brother, John, he became an assistant to his father in 1746. When John inherited the business upon their father's death, he brought first Robert and then another brother, James, into the firm, all becoming known as the Adam Brothers. He designed the mausoleum for his father in **Greyfriars Kirkyard** *Map p124* **P14** (1 Greyfriars Place, Adam family mausoleum, south-west corner, EH1 2QQ).

From 1755 to 1757, he went to Europe to study Roman architecture, making extensive drawings, and was arrested as a spy while taking measurements of the Emperor Diocletian's palace in Dalmatia, now in Croatia. Following his return to Britain, he set up the family business in London.

The prevailing architectural style was Palladian, based on the work of the Venetian architect Andrea Palladio, which Adam characterized as 'ponderous and disgustful'. Based on his research, he created the neoclassical or Georgian style, which he considered more flexible, also designing furniture and interiors to complement the buildings. Among the many Edinburgh buildings he designed are **Register House** *Map p122* **Q11** (HM General Register House, 2 Princes Street, EH1 3YY) and the north side of **Charlotte Square** *Map p120* **L12** (EH2 4DR).

He has been called Britain's most important neoclassical architect and possibly the most influential architect ever, building his success on his vision and his attention to detail. In 1792 he was appointed architect to King George III. He and his brothers designed buildings from Inverness to Brighton. A medallion is in the **Scottish National Portrait Gallery** *Map p122* **P10** (1 Queen Street, gallery 5, second floor, paste medallion, EH2 1JD) and an architectural model in the **National Museum of Scotland** *Map p124* **Q14** (Chambers Street, 'Scotland Transformed', level 3, middle of east wall, EH1 1JF). He is buried at Westminster Abbey.

Framed cut-paper model of the east front of the Old College, University of Edinburgh, National Museum of Scotland *Map p124* **Q14**.

~ JOHN BELLANY ~

1942–, PAINTER

John Bellany was born into a family of fishermen and boat builders at **18 Gosford Road** (off map, EH32 0HF) in Port Seton, near Edinburgh. The religious family also believed in the many local fishing superstitions. As a boy he drew boats obsessively. In 1960 he became the first person from Port Seton to go to **Edinburgh College of Art** Map p124 **O15** (74 Lauriston Place, EH3 9DF). He lived with three other students at **150 Rose Street Lane South** Map p122 **M12** (eastern section of lanes, west side near corner with Rose Street, EH2 4BB), where he enhanced its walls with murals. During the Edinburgh Festival of 1963, he and another student, Sandy Moffat, held an exhibition on the railings of **Castle Terrace** Map p124 **M13** (near corner of Lothian Road, EH1 2EW), and again in the 1965 festival put on an open-air show on the railings of the **Playfair Steps** Map p122 **P12** (east of the Scottish National Gallery, EH2 2EL). He married a fellow student, Helen Percy, before going to the Royal College in London in 1965.

He worked prolifically, with his paintings becoming darker after a visit to the site of the Buchenwald concentration camp, when he also became convinced that there was no loving god. This period of his life was marked by heavy drinking and divorce, which led to a nervous breakdown and a return to his parents' home in 1974. His self-destructive lifestyle also meant that by 1988 he needed a liver transplant, which gave him a 'renewed zest for life'. He created many self-portraits while recovering in hospital. His second wife had died, and he had remarried his first wife in 1986.

His large output is characterized by colourful but often menacing images of birds and animals, the fishing community and religious themes. People are often hybrids with birds or animals. He has been called one of Scotland's greatest living artists, showing internationally, with his work in many public galleries around the world. In Edinburgh it is in the collections of the **Scottish National Gallery of Modern Art** Map p120 **H12** (Modern One, 75 Belford Road, not always on display, EH4 3DR) and the **Scottish National Portrait Gallery** Map p122 **P10** (1 Queen Street, not on display, EH2 1JD). He now divides his time between Cambridge, Edinburgh and Italy.

The railings of the Playfair Steps, one of the first places John Bellany exhibited his paintings Map p122 **P12**.

DAME ELIZABETH BLACKADDER

1931–, PAINTER

Elizabeth Violet Blackadder was born in Falkirk. She came to Edinburgh in 1949 to study for a combined degree in fine art, awarded by **Edinburgh College of Art** Map p124 O15 (74 Lauriston Place, EH3 9DF), and the University of Edinburgh, where she won several travelling scholarships. Following her 1956 marriage to fellow artist John Houston, they lived upstairs from another artist and friend, Anne Redpath, q.v., at **7 London Street** Map p122 P9 (EH3 6LZ). She taught at Edinburgh College of Art for many years, before retiring in 1986 to devote herself full-time to painting and printmaking.

While she has done landscapes and portraits, Blackadder is best known for her water-colour still lives featuring flowers from her own garden, found or acquired objects and her cats. The disparate elements can appear to be scattered over the page, often more like botanical illustrations than traditional still lives. Trips to Japan have meant that Japanese objects are now included. She often uses Japanese paper and is inspired by the country's aesthetic sensibility, for example leaving significant amounts of empty space in her compositions.

Blackadder has many firsts to her name, including being the first woman elected to both the Royal Academy and the **Royal Scottish Academy** Map p122 O12 (The Mound, EH2 2EL) where a large retrospective of her work was held in 2011 and 2012, and being the first woman to be appointed Her Majesty's Painter and Limner in Scotland, a post held 200 years previously by Sir Henry Raeburn, q.v. She was created Dame Commander of the Most Excellent Order of the British Empire in 2003. Her work is in many national and international collections, including those of the Heriot-Watt University, the **Scottish National Gallery of Modern Art** Map p120 H12 (Modern One, 75 Belford Road, not always on display, EH4 3DR), and the University of Edinburgh. She has been called Scotland's best living female artist and is also one of the most popular, with reproductions of her flowers and cats on everything from mugs to tea towels. She has lived for many years in the Grange area of Edinburgh.

One of Elizabeth Blackadder's watercolour still lives (not on public display).

∽ Francis Cadell ∽

1883–1937, PAINTER

Francis Campbell Boileau Cadell was born at **4 Buckingham Terrace** Map p120 **J11** (EH4 3AB), the son of a surgeon. At sixteen he went to study in Paris at the Académie Julian, where he was impressed by the work of Matisse and the early Fauvists. He returned to Edinburgh in 1908, when he had his first solo show, after which he exhibited regularly in Scotland. He focused on landscapes, still lives and Edinburgh interiors, both in oil and water-colour. He is noted for his use of strong colour, loose style and the depiction of fashionable women.

During World War I, he served with two Scottish regiments and sketched fellow servicemen. Upon his return he became friends with another artist, Samuel Peploe, q.v., who was a strong influence on him, and travelled with him to Iona several times. With John Duncan Fergusson and Leslie Hunter, the four became known as the Scottish Colourists and they created a distinctive Scottish idiom. They were known for fresh colour, but not for daring subject matter. Cadell was initially successful, but his work fell out of favour by the 1930s, with sales also hit by the Great Depression. He lived at **6 Ainslie Place** Map p120 **L11** (EH3 6AR) and **22 Ainslie Place** Map p120 **L11** (EH3 6AJ), before moving in 1932 to **30 Regent Terrace** Map p118 **U10** (EH7 5BS). In ill health due to cirrhosis of the liver, he moved to more humble premises at **4 Warriston Crescent** Map p116 **N6** (EH3 5LA) in 1934 and died in poverty at

The Black Hat, Francis Cadell, collection of the City Art Centre (not on display) Map p122 **Q12**.

the **Officers Association Nursing Home** Map p120 **I11** (25 Belgrave Crescent, EH4 3AL). Although he was elected an academician of the Royal Scottish Academy in 1936, he had had to apply to their Fund for the Relief of Decayed Artists and had their uncashed cheque for £50 in his pocket at the time of his death. His paintings now sell for hundreds of thousands of pounds.

He is buried in the **Dean Cemetery** Map p120 **I11** (63 Dean Path, through Dean Path gates, turn left, first path on right, first path on left, towards end of path on left, EH4 3AT), and his work can be seen at the **National War Museum** Map p124 **N13** (Edinburgh Castle, Castlehill, EH1 2NG) and in the collection of the **City Art Centre** Map p122 **Q12** (2 Market Street, viewing by appointment, EH1 1DE).

～ JAMES CRAIG ～

1739–95, ARCHITECT

James Craig was the son of a merchant and went to **George Watson's Hospital** Map p124 **P16** (since demolished, near Peter's Yard café, 27 Simpson Loan, EH3 9GG), a school for the sons of 'deceased and indigent' merchants. He was then apprenticed in 1755 to a stonemason, qualifying after nine years, but does not appear to have had any architectural training.

In 1766 Edinburgh was an overcrowded, dirty and smelly city, largely confined to the Royal Mile and its immediate surroundings. The city fathers decided to hold a competition to design new suburbs to the north of the town, then open fields. Seven entries were received, and the young and unknown James Craig was the winner. His simple grid design for what became known as the New Town had broad streets for the wealthy and narrow lanes in between for servants and stables. Squares and statues were incorporated, all in a balanced structure. He also used the contours of the land to allow open vistas from both Princes Street and Queen Street. He travelled to London to study the latest sewer systems, and the city agreed to cobble the streets and install sewers and a water supply. Building work started in 1767 and was completed in 1820, with later additions up until the 1850s. The wealthy left the Old Town for this more healthy and spacious accommodation.

Craig went on to design other individual buildings and streets, including the **Assembly Rooms** Map p122 **O11** (54 George Street, EH2 2LR) and **Merchant Street** Map p124 **P14** (EH1 2QD). From 1773 until his death he lived at the foot of **West Bow** Map p124 **P14** (near 112 West Bow, corner of the Grassmarket, EH1 2HH). In later years he had little work, his patrons having died or lost power, and had financial difficulties, eventually dying insolvent. He is buried in **Greyfriars Kirkyard** Map p124 **P14** (1 Greyfriars Place, first path on right, EH1 2QQ).

The New Town (with the Old Town) was designated a UNESCO World Heritage Site in 1995. It is one of the largest extents of Georgian architecture in the world and one of the earliest examples of town planning. His plans can be seen in the **Museum of Edinburgh** Map p118 **T12** (Huntly House, 142 Canongate, Royal Mile, EH8 8DD) and the **National Museum of Scotland** Map p124 **Q14** (Chambers Street, 'Scotland Transformed', level 3, middle south, EH1 1JF).

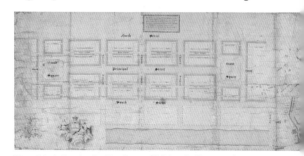

The original plans for the New Town of Edinburgh, Museum of Edinburgh Map p118 **T12**.

HILL AND ADAMSON

DAVID OCTAVIUS HILL, 1802–70, PAINTER AND PHOTOGRAPHER
ROBERT ADAMSON, 1821–48, PHOTOGRAPHER AND ENGINEER

David Octavius Hill was born in Perth and moved upon marriage to **19 Moray Place** *Map p120* **L11** (EH3 6DA). He was a landscape painter and book illustrator. Robert Adamson was born in St Andrews, where he had experimented with a new photographic process, the calotype. The advantages of the calotype over the more prevalent daguerreotype were that it required less exposure time and multiple copies could be made from it. From 1843 they collaborated in their photographic studio at **Rock House** *Map p118* **R11** (28 Calton Hill, near entrance to path off Regent Road leading up Calton Hill, left side, EH1 3BH), working both indoors and on the roof, which had views north and south. Hill contributed the artistic content, while Adamson provided the technical expertise. Their first project was to photograph every one of the 450 dissenting ministers who had participated in the schism, the 'Disruption' with the Church of Scotland, so that Hill could paint a composite picture. This mammoth task meant that he completed the painting only twenty-three years later. At the same time, they went on to take pictures of a huge range of subjects, from fisherfolk and soldiers to the famous of the day. Views and street scenes were also subjects. Together they created a total of around 3,000 prints.

The partnership lasted only four years, ending with Adamson's illness and untimely death. Hill had initially viewed photography only as an *aide-mémoire* for the painter, but the complementary talents of the partnership meant that they were able to take photography into another dimension. They had produced fine pictorial images, not merely documentary photos, and are regarded as the first to have turned photography into an art form.

Hill continued to live at Rock House after the death of Adamson, concentrating more on his painting, before moving to **Newington Lodge** *Map p128* **V20** (38 Mayfield Terrace, EH9 1RZ). A bust of Hill is in the **Scottish National Portrait Gallery** *Map p122* **P10** (1 Queen Street, bust in entrance hall, photos in Photography Gallery (not always on display), first floor, EH2 1JD), and

The gate at Rock House, Calton Hill, where Hill and Adamson had their photographic studio *Map p118* **R11**.

he is buried at **Dean Cemetery** *Map p120* **I11** (63 Dean Path, through Dean Path gates, turn left, first path on right, eighteenth monument on right-hand side, EH4 3AT). Their work is in the Scottish National Portrait Gallery, the **National War Museum** *Map p124* **N13** (Edinburgh Castle, Castlehill, photos on stairway between ground and first floor, EH1 2NG) and the collection of the **City Art Centre** *Map p122* **Q12** (2 Market Street, EH1 1DE, viewing by appointment).

～ John Kay ～

1742–1826, CARICATURIST

John Kay was born near Dalkeith and apprenticed to a barber there. In 1761 he moved into Edinburgh as a journeyman barber, and ten years later was a master of his trade, a surgeon-barber. At his shop he began to make miniature paintings and etchings of his clients, although he had no training in art. His skill attracted the patronage of Sir William Nisbet of Dirleton, upon whose death he was granted an annuity of £20. With this income and the increasing popularity of his prints, Kay gave up barbering in 1785 and opened a print shop in **Parliament Close** *Map p124* **Q13** (Old Parliament Close, since demolished, east side of St Giles Cathedral, Royal Mile, EH1 1RE).

These caricatures would gently mock their subjects, who ranged from the humblest to the highest-ranking in Edinburgh. However, some of those depicted did not enjoy being the butt of his humour. On at least one occasion he was beaten with a cudgel and was also prosecuted, albeit unsuccessfully. Others bought up the images of themselves only to destroy them.

Kay was lucky to live during the Scottish Enlightenment, when many prominent figures who are still household names walked the streets near his premises. Among his subjects were Adam Smith, q.v., James Hutton, q.v., and Deacon Brodie, q.v. It is estimated he made 900 images, with only about 340 having survived. He planned to publish them as a book, but this project was not realized until 1837, when the first of the eventual eight volumes of *Edinburgh Portraits* was published by Hugh Paton.

Kay lived at **227 High Street** *Map p124* **Q13** (Royal Mile, plaque at first-floor level, EH1 1PE) until the time of his death. He is buried in **Greyfriars Kirkyard** *Map p124* **P14** (1 Greyfriars Place, northwest corner, unmarked grave, EH1 2QQ). His caricatures are in the **Scottish National Portrait Gallery** *Map p122* **P10** (1 Queen Street, gallery 7, second floor, thirteen etchings, one oil self-portrait, EH2 1JD) and the **Museum of Edinburgh** *Map p118* **T12** (Huntly House, 142 Canongate, Royal Mile, first floor, etchings, EH8 8DD). His widow said, 'He cared for no employment except that of etching likenesses.' His eye for detail, coupled with his ability to home in on human frailties, make his portraits a unique record of the Edinburgh of his day.

John Kay's portrait of Adam Smith, Scottish National Portrait Gallery *Map p122* **P10**.

～ ALISON KINNAIRD ～

1949–, GLASS ARTIST AND HARPIST

Alison Margaret Kinnaird was born at **2 Rillbank Crescent** Map p128 **Q18** (EH9 1LJ). When she was five, the family moved to **45 Dick Place** Map p128 **Q21** (EH9 2JA) where there was a summer house in the garden, in which she was able to start doing glass engraving. However, her first training had been in music, playing the cello, then taking up the small Scottish harp at fourteen and becoming a founder member of the Edinburgh Youth Orchestra. Since then she has combined these two strands of creativity.

Following study at the University of Edinburgh, where she was awarded an MA in Celtic studies and archaeology, from the late 1960s Kinnaird started to take classes in glass engraving. After her marriage to fellow musician Robin Morton, they lived at **24 Hugh Miller Place** Map p116 **L8** (EH3 5JG). Using a variety of techniques from sandblasting to acid etching on crystal, she started to get commissions, ranging from trophies to a goblet that was presented to the Queen Mother. Her beautifully drawn images of humans were always monochrome, with colour featuring only later in her career. Commissions and sales on a larger scale followed, including one for the new **Scottish Parliament** Map p118 **U12** (Horse Wynd, entrance hall, EH99 1SP). In 2012 the Queen inaugurated the *Donor Window* at the **Scottish National Portrait Gallery** Map p122 **P10** (1 Queen Street, Donor Window, top of east stair; also portrait of Roy Dennis, ground floor, EH2 1JD), which includes a portrait of Her Majesty and those of twelve major benefactors.

As a harpist, Kinnaird plays and records traditional Scottish music, sometimes with the Battlefield Band, and does research into it, having authored several books. In 1979 her album, *The Harp Key – Crann nan Teud*, was the first recording of Scottish harp music. Her 1992 book, *Tree of Strings*, written in collaboration with Keith Sanger, was the first to document the history of the harp in Scotland. Other books help the novice harpist and contain Kinnaird's arrangements of tunes.

In 1997 Kinnaird was honoured with an MBE for services to art and music, one of several awards. Her glass is exhibited internationally, and her eight albums are widely respected.

Psalmsong, Alison Kinnaird's glass work of art in the Scottish Parliament Map p118 **U12**.

SIR EDUARDO PAOLOZZI

1924–2005, ARTIST

Eduardo Luigi Paolozzi was born at **6 Crown Place** *Map p118* **V4** (since demolished, near 39 Leith Walk, EH6 8LS), the son of Italian immigrants. The following year they moved to **12 Albert Street** *Map p118* **T7** (and shop at 10 Albert Street, EH7 5LG), where they lived above their ice-cream shop. As a teenager he attended **Holy Cross Academy** (off map, now St Augustine's RC High School, 208 Broomhouse Road, EH12 9AD). When Italy declared war on Britain in 1940, he was interned at **Saughton prison** (off map, HM Prison Edinburgh, 33 Stenhouse Road, EH11 3LN). During this time, his father, grandfather and uncle were among 446 interned British Italians drowned when the ship transporting them to Canada was sunk by a U-boat.

Paolozzi attended evening classes at **Edinburgh College of Art** *Map p124* **O15** (74 Lauriston Place, EH3 9DF) and used the studio of a friend, Norman Forrest, at **16 Regent Terrace** *Map p118* **T11** (EH7 5BN) before going to the Slade School of Fine Art in London and then to Paris, where he met surrealists and other artists. Although he didn't like the term 'pop', preferring to characterize himself as a surrealist, he was producing this type of art long before it was 'invented' by Andy Warhol. He enjoyed exploring American consumerist imagery in order to criticize it. Another frequent theme was the relationship between humans and machines, including robots. He worked in many media – prints, collage, mosaic, tapestry and even an album cover – but is primarily remembered as a sculptor, often working on a monumental scale.

In 1994 Paolozzi gave most of the contents of his studio and many of his works of art to the National Galleries of Scotland. In 1999 the **Dean Gallery** *Map p120* **H12** (now Modern Two, 73 Belford Road, recreation of studio, indoor and outdoor sculptures, EH4 3DS) was opened. It recreated his studio and displayed many of his works, along with those of other surrealist and Dada artists. His most prominent sculpture in Edinburgh is at **York Place** *Map p118* **R10** (Picardy

Part of Sir Eduardo Paolozzi's sculpture, *The Manuscript of Monte Cassino,* top of Leith Walk, Picardy Place *Map p118* **R10**.

Place roundabout, York Place, EH1 3JD). *The Manuscript of Monte Cassino* faces towards his birthplace, and also recalls both the area most Edinburgh Italians came from and the terrible World War II battle there. Its aim was to create peace amid chaos. One of the most prolific and respected artists of his day, he was knighted in 1988.

~ SAMUEL PEPLOE ~

1871–1935, PAINTER

Samuel John Peploe was born at **39 Manor Place** *Map p120* **J13** (EH3 7EB), with the family later moving to **14 George Street** *Map p122* **P11** (now The Dome pub, EH2 2PF). He studied at the **Collegiate School** *Map p122* **M12** (27–28 Charlotte Square, now National Trust for Scotland, EH2 4ET), before turning away from a conventional life in one of the professions to train as a painter in Edinburgh and Paris, the latter's artists becoming a lifelong inspiration to him. He particularly admired Edouard Manet and the Dutch master, Franz Hals. When he returned to Edinburgh, he and three other painters, Francis Cadell, q.v., John Duncan Fergusson and Leslie Hunter, together became known as the Scottish Colourists. The Colourists combined the influence of the important French artists of the day with Scottish traditions to create a unique Scottish style – a post-impressionism with strong and definite shapes, sometimes with angularities reminiscent of cubism, and a bold use of strong colour.

Peploe concentrated on landscapes and still lives, also doing some portraiture. He went on painting trips to France, lived in Paris for a time, and also travelled to paint in many parts of Scotland, including the Western Isles, sometimes accompanied by Cadell or Fergusson. His first solo show was in 1903 at the **Scottish Gallery** *Map p122* **O10** (16 Dundas Street, EH3 6HZ), and he went on to show in Paris and New York.

He lived with his elder brother at **8 Ravelston Terrace** *Map p120* **H11** (EH4 3EF), and later at **17 Belford Road** *Map p120* **J12** (EH4 3BL), before his marriage to Margaret Mackay in 1910. He was the only one of the Colourists to earn a decent income during his lifetime. His final home was at **13 India Street** *Map p122* **M10** (EH3 6HA).

Major retrospectives of the work of the Scottish Colourists have brought them more recent acclaim, with a Peploe now having sold for nearly one million pounds. His best-known works are still lives with flowers, in particular roses or tulips. In the novel *44 Scotland Street* by Alexander McCall Smith, q.v., part of the plot centres around the authenticity of a painting believed to be a Peploe.

White Roses and Grapes, Samuel Peploe, collection of the University of Edinburgh (not on display).

~ WILLIAM PLAYFAIR ~

1789–1857, ARCHITECT

William Henry Playfair was born in London, the son of an architect. His father died in 1794, and he was sent to Edinburgh to live with his uncle, Professor John Playfair, a prominent scientist and mathematician. After studying at the University of Edinburgh, he trained with the Glasgow architect William Starke. At the age of twenty-seven, he won the contract to complete Robert Adam's, q.v., plans for the **University of Edinburgh** Map p126 **R14** (Old College, South Bridge, plaque inside entrance on right, EH8 9YL) buildings, which he worked on between 1817 and 1824.

At the same time, from 1820 he was working on the **City Observatory** Map p118 **S11** (38 Calton Hill, access by stairs from Waterloo Place, from mini-roundabout on Regent Road or pathway from Royal Terrace, EH7 5AA), built in neoclassical style to look like a Greek temple. Another nearby structure was to be the **National Monument** Map p118 **S11** (Calton Hill, same access as City Observatory, EH7 5AA). In collaboration with another architect, Charles Robert Cockerell, he was to create a replica of the Parthenon as a memorial to those killed in the Napoleonic Wars. However, since it was never completed due to lack of funds, it has become known as Scotland's Disgrace.

Much of the New Town, originated by James Craig, q.v., owes its look to Playfair, particularly its eastern sections. He designed many of its terraces, and some individual buildings, such as **St Stephen's Church** Map p122 **M9** (now St Stephen's Centre, St Stephen Street, EH3 5AB). However, his overall plan for the extension of the New Town was never completed. Other prominent buildings include the **Royal Scottish Academy** Map p122 **O12** (The Mound, EH2 2EL) and **Surgeons' Hall** Map p126 **R14** (now Surgeons' Hall Museum, 18 Nicolson Street, EH8 9DW). Most of his architecture was in the Greek revival style, contributing to Edinburgh's sobriquet as the Athens of the North, although he could turn his hand to Gothic, Tudor and Italianate styles.

From 1831 until his death, Playfair lived and worked at **17 Great Stuart Street** Map p120 **L12** (EH3 7TP). He is buried in the **Dean Cemetery** Map p120 **I11** (63 Dean Path, through Dean Path gates, turn left, first path on right, to end, turn left, on right-hand side against wall, EH4 3AT), where he had also designed other monuments. As one of the greatest architects of the nineteenth century, he was responsible for some of the finest buildings in Edinburgh and much of the extension of the original New Town.

St Stephen's Church, designed by William Playfair Map p122 **M9**.

~ SIR HENRY RAEBURN ~

1756–1823, PAINTER

Henry Raeburn was born in Stockbridge, then a separate village near Edinburgh, the son of a yarn boiler, but both parents soon died. His older brother sent him to **Heriot's Hospital** Map p124 **P15** (now George Heriot's School, Lauriston Place, EH3 9EQ), and then he was apprenticed at age fifteen to a jeweller and goldsmith in **Parliament Close** Map p124 **Q13** (Old Parliament Close, east side of St Giles Cathedral, Royal Mile, since demolished, EH1 1RE). During this time he taught himself to make miniature portraits and sometime adorned the jewellery with them. He came to the notice of Scotland's leading portrait painter of the age, David Martin, who taught him how to paint and to establish himself in his own right.

In 1778 Raeburn was asked to paint the portrait of Ann Leslie, a wealthy young widow he had admired while out sketching. They married a month later, bringing Raeburn a fortune. They were able to travel to Italy so that he could study the work of the masters, before returning to settle at **Deanhaugh House** Map p120 **L9** (since demolished, south of Leslie Place, near EH4 1NG).

Raeburn was now much in demand and painted the images of most of the prominent people of the Scottish Enlightenment – Adam Smith, q.v., James Boswell, q.v., Sir Walter Scott, q.v., and many more. From 1789 until 1809 he lived, painted and displayed his portraits at **32 York Place** Map p122 **Q10** (plaque at first-floor level, EH1 3HU). At the same time he was a property developer, building streets of houses at Raeburn Place, Ann Street and Leslie Place in Stockbridge.

Raeburn became the foremost portrait painter of his era in Scotland. His work is typified by an insight into the character of the sitter and a sensitivity and sureness of brushstroke, highlighted by dramatic lighting. His robust style as well as his ability to put sitters at their ease made him popular and successful. Many of his works are in the **Scottish National Portrait Gallery** Map p122 **P10** (1 Queen Street, gallery 7, second floor, self-portrait, other portraits, medallion, bust, EH2 1JD) and the **Scottish National Gallery** Map p122 **O12** (The Mound, many portraits, EH2 2EL). He died at **St Bernard's House** Map p120 **L9** (since demolished, between Leslie Place and Dean Terrace, near Deanhaugh Street, near EH4 1LY) and is buried at the **Church of St John the Evangelist** Map p124 **M13** (cemetery entrance behind church off Princes Street, first enclosure on right, middle of north wall, sometimes locked, EH2 4BJ).

Raeburn's most famous work, *Rev. Dr Robert Walker Skating on Duddingston Loch*, Scottish National Gallery Map p122 **O12**.

~ Anne Redpath ~

1895–1965, PAINTER

Anne Redpath was born in the Scottish Borders town of Galashiels, the daughter of a tweed designer. Although she saw her artistic work as relating to her father's choice of colour in his, her parents didn't support her wish to study at **Edinburgh College of Art** *Map p124* **O15** (74 Lauriston Place, EH3 9DF). So she was obliged to combine her diploma with a qualification in teaching from Moray House College of Education. After graduation she took up a travelling bursary to visit Brussels, Bruges, Paris and Italy. She was inspired by Matisse and the Fauvists, in addition to the home-grown influences of Scottish Colourists Samuel Peploe, q.v., and Francis Cadell, q.v.

In 1920 she married the architect James Michie, and they lived in France for fifteen years while he worked for the War Graves Commission. They returned to her parents' home in the Borders in 1934, but her husband worked in London and elsewhere and hardly came home. She was perennially short of money, supporting herself and her three sons only through her painting.

She was frequently in Edinburgh, whether to exhibit her work or to go to parties at **International House** *Map p122* **N12** (118 Princes Street, corner of Castle Street, first floor, EH2 4AA), where she enjoyed the cosmopolitan atmosphere. She moved back to Edinburgh in 1949, sharing a house at **16 Mayfield Gardens** *Map p128* **U21** (upper flat, EH9 2BZ) with her grown-up son and his family. From 1952 until her death she lived and worked at **7 London Street** *Map p122* **P9** (carved in stone, left of door, EH3 6LZ).

Her work was always figurative, mainly landscapes and still lives. Her last fifteen years saw her doing her most powerful work, and this coincided with increased sales. In 1952 she was the first woman to be elected to the Royal Scottish Academy, and in 1955 she was awarded an OBE. Despite left-wing views, she had a taste for fashion, and with her increased success she indulged herself by buying an extravagant hat. Her paintings are in the collection of the **Scottish National Gallery of Modern Art** *Map p120* **H12** (Modern One, 75 Belford Road, not always on display, EH4 3DR) and many other galleries throughout Britain.

Treboul Harbour, Anne Redpath, collection of the University of Edinburgh (not on display).

PHOEBE TRAQUAIR

1852–1936, ARTIST

Phoebe Anna Moss was born near Dublin and moved upon marriage to Edinburgh, where the family lived at **8 Dean Park Crescent** Map p120 J10 (EH4 1PH). Her husband, a palaeontologist, wrote research papers, and she provided detailed drawings of fossils for him. Then while at home with a young family, she started doing domestic linen embroidery. From 1890 she worked in the **Dean Studios** Map p120 J12 (since demolished, beside Drumsheugh Swimming Baths, Belford Road, EH4 3BL), where she completed several illuminated manuscripts. Her first commission was for murals in the chapel of the **Sick Children's Hospital** Map p128 Q18 (now partly moved to the chapel of the Royal Hospital for Sick Children, Rillbank, EH9 1LU). She went on to create many more murals, the most well known of which is at the **Catholic Apostolic Church** Map p116 Q8 (now the Mansfield Traquair Centre, 15 Mansfield Place, by appointment, EH3 6BB). She also excelled in many other media, including leather tooling, enamel, jewellery and embroidery. Determined to be recognized as a professional artist, she signed her monogram on all her work. In 1920 she became the first, albeit honorary, woman member of the Royal Scottish Academy, having previously been refused membership.

As part of the Scottish Arts and Crafts movement, Traquair rejected a hierarchy in the arts, seeing equal value in both decorative and high art. Her work was always pictorial, with a balance between the real and imaginary. Like others in the Arts and Crafts movement, she believed that art should unite past and present and have a moral message and should therefore be a mixture of symbolism and realism. Christian imagery could be combined with references to Greek myths. Her influences came from the Pre-Raphaelites and medieval manuscripts and tapestries.

Her work can be seen in the **National Museum of Scotland** Map p124 Q14 (Chambers Street, level 5, south wall and west wall, and 'Inspired by Nature', EH1 1JF), and her four-panel embroidery masterpiece, *The Progress of a Soul*, is in the **Scottish National Gallery** Map p122 O12 (The Mound, EH2 2EL). A bust is in the **Scottish National Portrait Gallery** Map p122 P10 (1 Queen Street, gallery 9, second floor, EH2 1JD). She died at **The Bush, Colinton** (off map, 13 Spylaw Bank Road, EH13 0JW) and is buried at **Colinton Parish Church** (off map, Dell Road, EH13 0JR), beneath a stone she had designed. Traquair was the first significant professional Scottish woman artist of the modern era, particularly noted for her achievements in murals and textiles.

The Victory, the final panel of *The Progress of a Soul*, Scottish National Gallery Map p122 O12.

2

PERFORMERS

When Allan Ramsay founded a theatre in 1736, magistrates saw this as an outrageous act and summarily closed it down. It was only in the late nineteenth century that performers were to move back into prominence in Edinburgh. The first of these, Sir Harry Lauder, soon left for London, where he dressed as Sassenachs thought Highlanders dressed, and was a great music-hall success, performing comic turns and songs. Scots and comedy became linked in the public imagination.

Alastair Sim followed as the headmistress of the mythical St Trinian's, and later Ronnie Corbett would tell convoluted stories, often at his own expense. Sean Connery was an actor rather than a comedian, but his James Bond films enjoyed *double entendres* and were not to be taken entirely seriously.

Others have combined two or more careers in the public eye. Moira Shearer started off as a ballet dancer, then turned to acting. Magnus Magnusson was initially a journalist before finding fame as the presenter of the television quiz show, *Mastermind*.

Edinburgh is perhaps best known for its musicians, especially those connected with the folk revival of the 1960s and 1970s. Among those who were in at its beginnings were Roy Williamson, Aly Bain and Dick Gaughan. They combined superb musicianship with commitment, playing and singing their own compositions, interpretations of traditional ballads and the music of contemporaries. At the other end of the musical spectrum were the Bay City Rollers, Edinburgh's 1970s answer to an English group of four mop-top pop stars.

Today's crop of pop singers includes Shirley Manson, an alternative rock star, who combines singing with writing music. The actor Ken Stott is most closely connected with the television version of the glowering Inspector Rebus, the Ian Rankin detective who keeps Edinburgh safe from criminals.

Edinburgh has been the backdrop to many performances, not only in films such as *Chariots of Fire* and *Burke and Hare*, but also as a venue for comedians, actors and singers who returned to play in the old Empire Theatre, now the Festival Theatre, or one of its many other venues. Not to mention the Edinburgh International Festival, the Fringe, the Film Festival, the Book Festival, the Jazz Festival, etc., where thousands perform each year. The eighteenth-century magistrates would be apoplectic to discover that their attempts to separate Edinburgh from theatre, music and other performance have been completely in vain. Hosting the biggest arts festival in the world, Edinburgh and its many performers have happily overturned the archaic idea that it was all the work of the devil.

The Usher Hall, where many musicians and actors have plied their trade *Map p124* **M14**.

⌒ ALY BAIN ⌒

1946–, MUSICIAN

Alistair Bain was born in Shetland, the son of a cooper. At the age of eleven, he asked his parents to buy him a fiddle, which he initially learned to play from neighbours and the radio. From 1959 his teacher was Tom Anderson, who formed the Shetland Fiddlers Society. Bain's first public performance was in the following year for the Hamefaring, the homecoming for Shetlanders.

After leaving school at fifteen to become an apprentice baker, he was briefly a joiner, but left Shetland in 1968 with the aim of becoming a professional musician. He first stayed with his brother in Glasgow, where he formed the Humblebums with two other unknown musicians, Gerry Rafferty and Billy Connolly. In 1969 he moved to **47 Forrest Road** *Map p124* **Q15** (EH1 2QP), Edinburgh, and performed at the nearby **Forrest Hill Bar** *Map p124* **Q15** (now Sandy Bell's Bar, 25 Forrest Road, EH1 2QH), where he enjoyed the beginnings of the folk revival. In the same year he formed the instrumental group, Boys of the Lough, with three other musicians. Various members came and went, but the group, which was committed to traditional music, started to tour and had an album by 1972. International tours followed, with New York's Carnegie Hall the high point.

Bain is known for his virtuoso fiddle playing, with fast and difficult pieces his specialty. He has the ability to play with many different musicians, put brilliantly to use in the four series of *Transatlantic Sessions*, in which he played with traditional, classical and country musicians of every ilk. With Phil Cunningham, he is the mainstay of the BBC's annual Hogmanay programme from Edinburgh, broadcast from **West Princes Street Gardens** *Map p124* **N13** (EH2 2HG). They also performed at the 1999 opening of the devolved Scottish Parliament *Map p118* **U12** (Horse Wynd, EH99 1SP). His own record label is **Whirlie Records** *Map p122* **Q9** (14 Broughton Place, EH1 3RX).

Bain has helped younger generations of musicians by conceiving the idea for the Heritage of Scotland Summer School at Stirling University and has played with young, new musicians on tour. He has received many honours for his work.

Sandy Bell's, where many folk musicians including Aly Bain have honed their craft *Map p124* **Q15**.

～ BAY CITY ROLLERS ～

1969–78, POP GROUP

The Bay City Rollers were a pop group formed by Eric Falconer, Stuart 'Woody' Wood, Les McKeown, and brothers Alan and Derek Longmuir. They were born respectively at **11 Arthur Street** *Map p118* **T6** (EH6 5DA), **4 Marchmont Street** *Map p128* **N18** (EH9 1EJ), **8 Broomhouse Medway** (off map, EH11 3RP), **5 Caledonian Road** *Map p120* **J15** (EH11 2DA) and **20 Smithfield Street** *Map p128* **E18** (EH11 2PQ). They chose their name by throwing a dart, which landed near Bay City, Michigan, on a map of America. Most popular with fourteen-year-old teenyboppers, they wore characteristic outfits featuring short, wide trousers, often with tartan cuffs, tartan scarves, striped socks and platform shoes. Their most famous hits were 'Keep on Dancing', 1971, and 'Shang-a-Lang' in 1974.

The Longmuir brothers, who started their musical career at **Tynecastle High School** *Map p128* **F17** (2 McLeod Street, EH11 2ND) had founded a band called The Saxons in about 1969, with Alan, who became a plumber, on guitar and Derek, a joiner, on drums, and a school friend, Nobby Clark, on vocals. Clark and others joined and left the group until, by 1974, the 'classic line-up' of the five was settled. They played at Edinburgh clubs until they were spotted by Tom Paton, who became their manager and was instrumental in branding and promoting them. Their squeaky-clean image, with innocent good looks, were soon subject to teen hysteria, when they would be mobbed by screaming girls.

After their singles went to number one, they went on international sell-out tours and had their own television show, *Shang-a-Lang*. Many of their hits were covers, but they also wrote their own songs, including 'Money Honey'. Although the height of their success was in the mid-1970s, when Rollermania meant that they were worldwide stars, their albums continue to sell into the twenty-first century. The band split up in 1978, but versions of it continued with names such as The Rollers, New Rollers and Les McKeown's Legendary Bay City Rollers. Estimates of their total sales range from 70 to 300 million records. The **National Museum of Scotland** *Map p124* **Q14** (Chambers Street, 'Scotland, a Changing Nation', level 6, north-west section, EH1 1JF) has memorabilia.

Detail of tartan trousers made by a fan in homage to the Bay City Rollers, National Museum of Scotland *Map p124* **Q14**.

⁓ SIR SEAN CONNERY ⁓

1930–, ACTOR

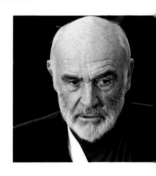

Thomas Sean Connery was born at **176 Fountainbridge** *Map p120* **K16** (since demolished, now 2 Melvin Walk, plaque near Fountainbridge, EH3 8EQ). His impoverished family sent the young boy to work delivering milk by horse-drawn cart for the **St Cuthbert's Cooperative Society** *Map p120* **L16** (92–98 Fountainbridge, now café, EH3 9QA). He attended **Bruntsfield Primary School** *Map p128* **L19** (Montpelier, EH10 4NA) and **Darroch Secondary School** *Map p128* **M17** (now Darroch Centre, 7 Gillespie Street, corner of Upper Gilmore Place, EH3 9NH) before joining the Royal Navy at sixteen, but lasted only three years because of stomach ulcers. Returning to Edinburgh, he did a series of dead-end jobs, lifeguarding at **Portobello Swimming Baths** (off map, now Portobello Swim Centre, 57 Promenade, EH15 2BS), polishing coffins and posing as an almost-nude life model at **Edinburgh College of Art** *Map p124* **O15** (74 Lauriston Place, EH3 9DF). His obsession with bodybuilding helped to launch his career, when he was placed third in one of the classes of the Mr Universe contest of 1953.

For years he had to make do with modelling and bit parts, until in 1958 he was cast opposite Lana Turner in *Another Time, Another Place*. It still took another four years until he overcame strong competition to become James Bond in *Dr. No*, the start of a glittering career which included six more Bond films, as well as numerous others. He won an Academy Award for Best Supporting Actor for his role in *The Untouchables* in 1987 and was named Sexiest Man Alive by *People* magazine in 1989.

Connery lives in Spain but maintains strong links to Edinburgh, where he has been made a freeman of the city. He donated the $1 million fee from one of his Bond films to found the Scottish International Education Trust, dedicated to helping Scots to develop their talents. He was knighted in 2000, delayed because of his support for Scottish independence.

Twice married, first to the actress Diane Cilento, and since 1975 to the French-Moroccan artist Micheline Roquebrune, he has retired as an actor. Despite his long and varied career, to his many fans he is best remembered as 007, the suave secret agent who liked it 'shaken not stirred'.

The Lady Lawson Street entrance to Edinburgh College of Art, where Sean Connery posed for students *Map p124* **O15**.

⟋ RONNIE CORBETT ⟍

1930–, COMEDIAN

Ronald Balfour Corbett was born at **22 Warrender Park Road** *Map p128* **N18** (EH9 1JG), the son of a baker. He attended **James Gillespie's School** *Map p128* **N18** (22–32 Warrender Park Crescent, now university student residences, EH9 1DY) and the **Royal High School** *Map p118* **T11** (Old Royal High School, 5–7 Regent Road, EH1 3DG), where he was stage-struck from an early age. He enrolled in an acting school, **Glover Turner Robertson School of Drama** *Map p122* **M12** (was above 135 George Street, EH2 4JS), where he worked on losing his Scottish accent. At sixteen he was the wicked aunt in *Babes in the Wood* at the youth club of **St Catherine's Church** *Map p128* **Q19** (St Catherine's Argyle Parish Church of Scotland, 61–63 Grange Road, EH9 1TY), and played the organ at churches around Edinburgh. He went to the theatre every week and would wait at the stage doors of the Royal Lyceum or the King's Theatre to meet the stars, or go to the **Regal Cinema** *Map p124* **M15** (now the Odeon Lothian Road, 118 Lothian Road, EH3 8BQ). In the eighteen months' gap after finishing school and before National Service, he decided on a job in the civil service, where he joined its amateur dramatics society and was assistant stage manager when they performed at the **Cygnet Theatre** *Map p126* **T16** (30 St Leonard's Street, since demolished, now site of St Leonards Police Station, EH8 9QW).

After National Service, he was determined to become an actor and left for London with £97 in his pocket. He has worked since the 1950s in show business, in cabaret, working with Danny La Rue, and in television in *The Frost Report*. His theatre roles include starring in the musical, *The Boys From Syracuse*, with many television appearances, most notably in *Sorry!*, a long-running 1980s sitcom in which he was an adult son dominated by his mother. Most famously he collaborated with Ronnie Barker as *The Two Ronnies* from 1971 until 1987. At 5'1", he often makes self-deprecating remarks about his size and has played roles much younger than his age.

Corbett specializes in rambling monologues with many digressions, often appearing to lose the plot. His gentle humour also relies on plays on words. 'A cement mixer has collided with a prison van. Motorists are asked to look out for sixteen hardened criminals.' He has been honoured with a CBE and lives in London.

~ Dick Gaughan ~

1948–, FOLK SINGER

Richard Peter Gaughan (rhymes with loch-an) was born in Glasgow, but only because his father was working there temporarily. The family soon returned to Leith, where his father came from, living at **6 Graham Street** *Map p118* **R3** (since demolished, near EH6 5QS) in less-than-ideal and sometimes even poor circumstances. His mother and paternal grandparents were amateur musicians in the folk tradition, and so Gaughan grew up immersed in Scottish and Irish music and started playing the guitar aged seven. He has been a professional musician and singer since 1970, concentrating on folk and Celtic music. Also, working in the background, he has been a session musician, music engineer and composer of film scores and songs recorded by other celebrated musicians such as Billy Bragg and Christy Moore.

In 1969 he and Aly Bain, q.v., were founder members of the Boys of the Lough, when both were living at **47 Forrest Road** *Map p124* **Q15** (EH1 2QP). With the folk revival in full swing, they played sessions at the nearby **Forrest Hill Bar** *Map p124* **Q15** (now Sandy Bell's Bar, 25 Forrest Road, EH1 2QH) and went on to make three albums with Gaughan on vocals. Since then Gaughan has pursued a solo career, interspersed with working with bands Five Hand Reel and Clan Alba, playing Edinburgh venues from the humble Leith Folk Club to the far grander **Queen's Hall** *Map p128* **S17** (85–89 Clerk Street, EH8 9JG) where he recorded a live

solo album during the 1984 Edinburgh International Festival. Still writing in many idioms, his most ambitious piece to date has been the ninety-minute orchestral work, *Timewaves – Lovesong to a People's Music*, first performed in 2004.

Gaughan has been called the Scottish Woody Guthrie for his performances of traditional ballads with his own, often political, compositions and for his championing of the rights and concerns of ordinary people. A member of the agit-prop theatre company, 7:84, in its heyday, he also played at the Dalkeith Miners' Welfare Club in support of the miners' strike of the mid-1980s. He has been the subject of two BBC documentaries and continues to tour internationally.

Queen's Hall, one of the venues Dick Gaughan has played *Map p128* **S17**.

～ SIR HARRY LAUDER ～

1870–1950, SINGER AND MUSIC HALL ENTERTAINER

Henry Lauder was born at the home of his grandfather at **3 Bridge Street, Portobello** (off map, plaque, EH15 1DB), the eldest of eight children. They moved to **Veitch's Cottages, Musselburgh** (off map, since demolished, grounds of Musselburgh Grammar School, 86 Inveresk Road, Musselburgh, EH21 7BA), when he was still a baby. Since his father was sometimes in ill health, he was sent to work from a young age, caddying at the **Musselburgh Links** (off map, Balcarres Road, Musselburgh, EH21 7SR). They later lived at **Brown's Buildings** (off map, since demolished, near 7 Rothesay Place, Musselburgh, EH21 7EX).

In 1882 the family moved to England, where his father died. His mother took her children to Arbroath where Lauder worked in a flax mill, went to school half-time and joined the Band of Hope, a Christian temperance society, where he learned to sing. At thirteen he won a competition. The following year the family moved again, this time to Hamilton, where he became a miner and also made his professional debut, earning five shillings.

He started to work in music hall, writing his own songs and doing comic turns, and by 1894 he was a professional, touring Scotland. When he went to London to seek his fortune in 1900, he got his big break when he stood in for an act who was ill. He enhanced his individuality by dressing in an exaggerated Highland outfit. In 1907 he made the first of twenty-two tours to North America and became the highest-paid performer in the world.

When his only son was killed during World War I, he wrote 'Keep Right on to the End of the Road' in his honour and began entertaining the troops and raising money for ex-servicemen. For this he was knighted, and in 1927 he was also granted the Freedom of the City of Edinburgh at the **Usher Hall** *Map p124* **M14** (Lothian Road, EH1 2EA). He continued to tour, appearing at the **Empire Palace Theatre** *Map p126* **R14** (now Festival Theatre, 13–29 Nicolson Street, EH8 9FT).

Lauder is remembered for songs including 'A Wee Deoch-an-Doris' and 'Roamin' in the Gloamin'', his gentle humour and his knobbly walking sticks. He is commemorated at the **National Museum of Scotland** *Map p124* **Q14** (Chambers Street, 'Scotland, a Changing Nation', level 6, north-west section, record album, EH1 1JF) and at **Portobello Town Hall** (off map, 147–149 Portobello High Street, Sir Harry Lauder memorial garden, EH15 2AW).

A copy of Sir Harry Lauder's *Keep Right on to the End of the Road*, National Museum of Scotland *Map p124* **Q14**.

MAGNUS MAGNUSSON

1929–2007, TV PERSONALITY

Magnus Magnusson was born in Iceland, but came to Edinburgh as a baby, living at **3 John Street, Portobello** (off map, EH15 2ED). His father had accepted a job with the Icelandic Cooperative, later becoming Consul-General of Iceland. Educated at the **Edinburgh Academy** Map p116 **M8** (42 Henderson Row, includes Magnusson Performing Arts Centre, EH3 5BL), where he was dux in 1948, he went on to Jesus College, Oxford, on a scholarship. While still a student, he wrote a column on DIY for the *Edinburgh Evening Dispatch*, despite knowing nothing about the subject. Every week he would bone up on the next topic in the college library.

In 1953 he started working for the *Scottish Daily Express*, then in 1961 he was head-hunted by *The Scotsman* newspaper Map p122 **Q12** (now the Scotsman Hotel, 20 North Bridge, EH1 1TR) for the position of chief feature writer, later rising to become assistant editor. At the same time, he began to freelance in broadcast journalism, presenting programmes at first on current affairs and later on history and the environment. He achieved real fame when he started hosting a new programme, the quiz show *Mastermind*, which he chaired for twenty-five years from 1972 until 1997 – it is still going strong, but with other presenters. In it he would ask contestants, who were seated in a black leather chair, questions on their specialist subject and on general knowledge. At its height it was watched by twenty million viewers. He was named Scottish television personality of the year in 1974.

Magnusson maintained an interest in Icelandic, Norse and Celtic culture and history, writing prolifically and translating from the Icelandic and Old Norse. He never took British citizenship and so received a knighthood from Iceland but could have only an honorary knighthood in Britain. A further honour was being elected rector of the **University of Edinburgh** Map p126 **R14** (Old College, South Bridge, EH8 9YL) in 1975.

Magnusson was talented in many areas, but he will always be associated in the public imagination with *Mastermind*. His catch-phrase, used when the final bleeps occurred during a question to a contestant, 'I've started, so I'll finish', has entered into popular culture.

Edinburgh Academy, where Magnus Magnusson was dux, and where a new building is named the Magnusson Performing Arts Centre
Map p116 **M8**.

~ Shirley Manson ~

1966–, SINGER

Shirley Ann Manson was born at **40a Northumberland Street** *Map p122* O10 (EH3 6JA), the daughter of a lecturer and a big-band singer. As a child, she was inspired by female classic jazz singers. At **Broughton High School** *Map p116* I8 (29 East Fettes Avenue, EH4 1EG) she became involved in drama and singing, appearing in several school productions. She was the member of a troupe that performed at the Edinburgh Festival Fringe in 1981, winning a Fringe First. During this time she and her family lived at **34 Comely Bank**

Map p120 I9 (EH4 1AJ), and she attended **Stockbridge Parish Church** *Map p116* M8 (7B Saxe Coburg Street, EH3 5BN) until she rejected it at the age of twelve, but returned there to get married in 1996.

Manson worked as a shop assistant at **Miss Selfridge** *Map p122* O12 (13–21 Hanover Street, EH2 2DL) for five years and modelled for *Jackie* magazine while pursuing a career in pop music, variously on lead vocals, as a backing singer, playing keyboard and writing music. In Britain, her first significant groups were Goodbye Mr Mackenzie and Angelfish, before she was spotted by Steve Marker of the American alternative rock band, Garbage. Their 1995 first album, *Garbage*, with Manson on lead vocals and guitar, sold four million copies, making her famous, especially after the band toured through 1996. She wrote much of the second album, which did equally well, and they also performed the theme song for the James Bond film, *The World is Not Enough*. The band's music is described as alternative, post-grunge and electronic.

Manson had a period of looking for a new direction, during which time she tried to write a solo album, and considered acting and giving up music. Some of her dilemmas were prompted by the death of her mother from dementia at a young age. However, she returned to music, citing its power to sustain even those in distress, and has performed with many other current top artists. She spent much of her career commuting between Edinburgh and the USA, but now lives permanently in Los Angeles.

MOIRA SHEARER

1926–2006, DANCER AND ACTOR

Moira Shearer King was born in Dunfermline, but was taken to Rhodesia, now Zimbabwe, at the age of six. There she learned to dance under the tutelage of a former member of Sergei Diaghilev's Ballets Russes. When the family returned to Britain, she trained at the Sadler's Wells School, making her stage debut as a fourteen-year-old student. She went on to leading roles, but she became internationally famous when she starred in the 1948 film *The Red Shoes*, based on the Hans Christian Andersen story of a young woman forced by her shoes to dance to death. She and the film helped to bring ballet to a new audience.

The following year, she was presenting prizes at a fancy dress ball, when Ludovic Kennedy, q.v., asked her to dance. She accepted, but said, 'I don't dance very well,' and went on to prove it by treading on his toes and nearly tripping him up. Despite this unpromising start, they were married in 1950.

Shearer soon retired from dancing, because of injury and a desire to turn to acting. One of her roles was as Titania in a 1954 Edinburgh Festival performance of *A Midsummer Night's Dream* at the **Empire Theatre** Map p126 **R14** (now Festival Theatre, 13–29 Nicolson Street, EH8 9FT), where she had previously danced when on tour with Sadler's Wells. The Old Vic production went on to tour in North America. She starred in several films, the most controversial of which was Michael Powell's *Peeping Tom*, a psychological thriller whose subject was voyeurism. In the 1970s, Edinburgh appearances included presenting the Eurovision Song Contest from the **Usher Hall** Map p124 **M14** (Lothian Road, EH1 2EA), much

to the amusement of her children, and playing in Noël Coward's *Hay Fever* at the **Royal Lyceum Theatre** Map p124 **M14** (Grindlay Street, EH3 9AX).

She and her family lived at **3 Upper Dean Terrace** Map p120 **K10** (EH4 1NU) before moving to England. The ballet shoes she wore in *The Red Shoes* are in the **National Museum of Scotland** Map p124 **Q14** (Chambers Street, 'Scotland, a Changing Nation', level 6, north-west section, EH1 1JF).

The ballet shoes worn by Moira Shearer in the film, *The Red Shoes*, National Museum of Scotland Map p124 **Q14**.

～ ALASTAIR SIM ～

1900–76, ACTOR

Alastair George Bell Sim was born above his father's tailor's shop at **96–98 Lothian Road** *Map p124* **M14** (plaque on Filmhouse, near left-hand entrance, EH3 9BZ). He attended **Bruntsfield Primary School** *Map p128* **L19** (Montpelier, EH10 4NA) and **James Gillespie's School** *Map p128* **N18** (22–32 Warrender Park Crescent, now university student residences, EH9 1DY), where he showed a love of the spoken word and mimicry, before leaving at fourteen to become an apprentice messenger for his father. He was briefly at the University of Edinburgh before he decided to become an actor, much to his parents' disapproval, while still living with them at **47 Pentland Terrace** (off map, EH10 6HD). He did teacher training at Moray House College of Education and was appointed to the Fulton Lectureship in Elocution at the University of Edinburgh in 1925.

At the same time he set up a children's school of drama and speech training at **5 Manor Place** *Map p120* **K14** (EH3 7DH), which was an immediate success. In 1926 he met his future wife, Naomi Plaskitt, there when he was twenty-six and she was twelve. They married when she turned eighteen.

In 1930, he gave up the school and his university post to try his luck in London. He had early successes as a stage actor in the classics, but he will be best remembered as both the headmistress and her ne'er-do-well brother in the 1954 film *The Belles of St Trinian's*, and several sequels, featuring out-of-control and rampaging schoolgirls. It was loosely based on the real **St Trinnean's School for Girls** *Map p128* **P19** (10 Palmerston Road, corner of Beaufort Road, 1922–25, EH9 1TN) and *Map p128* **V17** (St Leonard's House, 1925–46, now St Leonard's Hall, Pollock Halls of Residence, University of Edinburgh, 18 Holyrood Park Road, EH16 5AY). He was also memorable in the title role in the film *Scrooge*, 1951, and as Dr Robert Knox, q.v., in *The Anatomist*, both a play and a film.

He was elected rector of the University of Edinburgh in 1948 and awarded a CBE in 1953. He was an idiosyncratic master of comedy, whether as a buffoon or as Captain Hook, but he was also an intensely private man, refusing to sign autographs or give interviews. He believed he should be judged only on his performances, and his best are considered brilliant.

Plaque near where Alastair Sim was born, Filmhouse, Lothian Road *Map p124* **M14**.

KEN STOTT

1954–, ACTOR

Kenneth Campbell Stott was born at **19 St Leonard's Bank** Map p126 **T16** (EH8 9SQ), a few minutes' walk from St Leonards Police Station. He went to **George Heriot's School** Map p124 **P15** (Lauriston Place, EH3 9EQ), and as a teenager he was in a band called Keyhole with some of those who would go on to become the Bay City Rollers, q.v. He went to London to study acting and then worked primarily in the theatre, before some television appearances, supplementing his meagre income during this period by selling double-glazing.

In 1994 he was cast as the slightly creepy Detective Inspector McCall in the film *Shallow Grave*, set in Edinburgh. He played a police officer on the trail of the flatmates who had concealed the death of their newly arrived lodger and stolen his suitcase full of cash. The external shots for the flat inhabited by the central characters were at **6 North East Circus Place** Map p122 **N9** (EH3 6SP). Stott made his breakthrough in 2006 when he got the role of DI John Rebus in the television adaptation of the crime novels of Ian Rankin, q.v., whose protagonist is the Edinburgh detective. Rebus is a moral person, although his choice of female company often lacks judgement, and he has few other interests apart from smoking and drinking. One of his haunts is the **Oxford Bar** Map p122 **M11** (8 Young Street, EH2 4JB). His base at St Leonards Police Station is represented in external shots by **Waverley Court** Map p118 **R12** (City of Edinburgh Council headquarters building, 4 East Market Street, EH8 8BG), and the outside of his flat by **97 St Stephen Street** Map p122 **M9** (EH3 5AB).

Stott continues to work in the theatre, with roles in London's West End and on Broadway, as well as doing voice-overs, television and film work, often with a crime theme. He played Adolf Hitler in a 2005 television drama, *Uncle Adolf*.

While Stott himself supports Edinburgh's Heart of Midlothian football club (Hearts), Rebus supports Hibernian (Hibs). Stott has said this part of his role has been 'more difficult to do than to play Hitler'.

Waverley Court, the administrative headquarters of the City of Edinburgh Council, used as a stand-in for St Leonards Police Station Map p118 **R12**.

~ Roy Williamson ~

1936–90. SINGER AND SONGWRITER

Roy Murdoch Buchanan Williamson was born at **4 Royal Circus** *Map p122* **M9** (EH3 6SR). His father, an advocate, died when he was eight. The family then lived at **62 Northumberland Street** *Map p122* **N10** (EH3 6JE), where his musical mother fostered his talents in music.

He went on to **Edinburgh College of Art** *Map p124* **O15** (74 Lauriston Place, EH3 9DF), where he studied from 1955 until 1959, and formed a folk group with fellow student Ronnie Browne. He married another fellow student,

Violet Thomson, in 1958 and they went to live at **18 Fettes Row** *Map p122* **N9** (EH3 6RH) where two daughters were born. In the early 1960s they moved to **69 Northumberland Street** *Map p122* **N10** (EH3 6JG), to be near his mother. After teacher training at Moray House College of Education, he taught at Liberton School until 1964.

He continued to play the guitar with his group, and then invented a new instrument, the combolin, a combination of guitar, bass guitar and mandolin. The Corrie Folk Trio was formed in 1961, which became the Corries in 1965 with the original two members. They first appeared at the **Waverley Bar** *Map p126* **R13** (3–5 St Mary's Street, EH1 1TA) with Williamson as the instrumentalist and Browne as the singer. So successful were they that, by 1964, they were able to give up their day jobs to devote their time to songwriting and touring internationally. Records and television appearances followed.

Williamson and his family were now living at **17 Stirling Road** *Map p116* **L1** (EH5 3JA). After the break-up of his marriage, the house was also split, and he lived in its upper part, **8 Zetland Place** *Map p116* **L1** (EH5 3LY) before moving to Forres in the Highlands in the late 1970s. He died of a brain tumour there.

The Corries were part of the Scottish folk music revival, with the Scottish themes of their music speaking to Williamson's nationalism. His most famous composition, 'Flower of Scotland', went into the pop charts and is considered the unofficial Scottish national anthem. A fan's scrapbook about the Corries is in the **National Museum of Scotland** *Map p124* **Q14** (Chambers Street, 'Scotland, a Changing Nation', level 6, north-west section, EH1 1JF).

Scrapbook by a fan of the Corries, National Museum of Scotland
Map p124 **Q14**.

3

WRITERS

Poets, authors of novels and short stories, those dedicated to biography and autobiography, romance, horror, humour or detective fiction, literary criticism or history – all made their homes in Edinburgh and still do. The neighbourhood inhabited by Ian Rankin, Alexander McCall Smith and J. K. Rowling is humorously known as Writers' Block.

One particular genre that has been popular with authors and readers is variously known as detective, crime, mystery or police-procedural fiction. Robert Louis Stevenson started the trend, with his dark tales of the duality of human nature or betrayal, some of which were perhaps inspired by the real-life criminal, Deacon Brodie. Following shortly afterwards was Arthur Conan Doyle, who created a timeless character in Sherlock Holmes. Conan Doyle is known to have used his medical school tutor, Dr Joseph Bell, and the tales of a real Edinburgh detective, James McLevy, as inspiration. Today's authors, such as Kate Atkinson and Ian Rankin, keep crime fiction alive and often set their tales in Edinburgh.

Poetry has been part of Edinburgh life from at least the time of the first poet listed here, Allan Ramsay. In the early eighteenth century, he was fascinated by street life and went on to inspire Robert Fergusson and Scotland's national poet, Robert Burns. They all valued the vernacular tongue, using the voices of the lowliest of Edinburgh's inhabitants.

The earliest of the authors in this section is James Boswell, famous for his biography, the *Life of Samuel Johnson*. He was also an early travel writer and diarist, the latter being so racy, his descendants tried to suppress it. Thomas de Quincey also wrote honestly about himself in *Confessions of an English Opium-Eater*. However, Sir Walter Scott favoured the less realistic, with historical romances about heroes such as Rob Roy and Ivanhoe. More recently, Dorothy Dunnett wrote in the same vein, and now J. K. Rowling writes fantasy that delights both children and adults.

Edinburgh is the real setting for many works of fiction, from the prim girls' school in *The Prime of Miss Jean Brodie* by Muriel Spark to Irvine Welsh's *Trainspotting*, with its depiction of the world of drugs and despair. Fictional characters such as Inspector Rebus also have favourite haunts that are real Edinburgh places. Alexander McCall Smith goes a step further by including living Edinburgh people in his *44 Scotland Street* series. But whether Edinburgh is mentioned in the text or not, it is a place famed for its writers and the fictional characters who roam its streets.

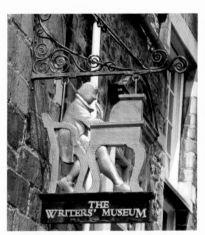

The sign at the Writers' Museum, devoted to the work of Sir Walter Scott, Robert Louis Stevenson and Robbie Burns, as well as many other Scottish writers
Map p124 **P13**.

KATE ATKINSON

1951–, WRITER

Kathrine Atkinson was born in York and studied at the University of Dundee, where she was awarded an MA in English literature. Keeping body and soul together by working in a range of jobs from legal secretary to teacher, she lived in Whitby, North Yorkshire, before settling in Edinburgh. She began writing in 1981, contributing to women's magazines. Her first novel, *Behind the Scenes at the Museum*, was published in 1995 and won the Whitbread Book Award, going on to become a bestseller.

Atkinson wrote more novels, then turned to crime fiction, several of which are set in and around Edinburgh, with former police inspector and now private detective Jackson Brodie the protagonist. In *One Good Turn*, Brodie sees or thinks he sees a body in the water near Cramond Island, nearly drowns and is rescued and taken to the nearby **Cramond Inn** (off map, 30 Cramond Glebe Road, EH4 6NU). Another character, the writer Martin Canning, visits the **Edinburgh International Book Festival** Map p122 **M12** (5A Charlotte Square, EH2 4DR), an event Atkinson herself has often participated in. With the Edinburgh Festival as the background setting, a Russian circus is performing in **The Meadows** Map p128 **Q17** (EH9 1LB). In *When Will There be Good News?* the accident-prone or possibly violence-magnet Brodie is taken to the **Royal Infirmary of Edinburgh** (off map, 51 Little France Crescent, EH16 4SA) following a train derailment at Musselburgh.

The first three Jackson Brodie novels were adapted and turned into a 2011 BBC television series starring Jason Isaacs, under the title *Case Histories*. The exterior of the first floor of **India Buildings** Map p124 **P13** (1–2 Victoria Street, EH1 2EX) was used as the fictional premises for Brodie's ramshackle office.

Atkinson's writing is characterized by twists and turns of plot, lots of coincidences, wit and humour and literary references. It is often bleak, with violence and murders aplenty, but with satisfyingly happy endings. Besides the novels, she has written short stories and plays, two of which were for the **Traverse Theatre** Map p124 **M14** (10 Cambridge Street, EH1 2ED). She has been awarded an MBE and lives in the Grange area of Edinburgh.

The first floor of India Buildings, Victoria Street, used for exterior shots of Jackson Brodie's office in *Case Histories* Map p124 **P13**.

~ HELEN BANNERMAN ~

1862–1946, WRITER AND ILLUSTRATOR

WRITERS

Helen Brodie Cowan Watson was born in her great-grandfather's house at **35 Royal Terrace** *Map p118* **T10** (EH7 5AH), one of seven children of a Free Church minister and his wife. She spent her early childhood in Madeira, where her father was posted, before they returned to Edinburgh in 1874. She studied at St Andrew's University. In 1889 she married Will Bannerman, a doctor in the Indian Medical Service and moved to India, where they lived in various postings, in particular Madras, now Chennai, and Bombay, now Mumbai, for thirty-two years. She wrote and illustrated *The Story of Little Black Sambo* for her two daughters. Set in an imaginary place with Indian and African aspects, it tells of a small boy who uses his ingenuity to outwit tigers who are intent on eating him. They chase each other around a tree until they turn into butter, which he takes home to be made into striped pancakes.

The story was published in 1899 and was an immediate success, but Bannerman lost control of the copyright, and many unauthorized editions were published with unpleasant, even racist, illustrations. She wrote eight other children's stories, but none was as successful, although some of them became school readers. The controversy about *Little Black Sambo* being derogatory to black people started only after her death. The common use of Sambo as a racist epithet was a later occurrence.

Her children were sent home to Edinburgh to live with their aunt at **50 Ann Street** *Map p120* **K10** (EH4 1PJ), the two girls in 1902 and the two boys in 1907, to continue their schooling. Her husband worked on a plague vaccine and retired in 1918 as Surgeon General of Madras, at which time they returned to Edinburgh. She died at her daughter's house at **11 Strathearn Place** *Map p128* **M20** (EH9 2AL), having been bedridden for seven years following a stroke. She is buried at the **Grange Cemetery** *Map p128* **P20** (60a Grange Road, north-west part of cemetery, section G, tall obelisk near large sycamore, EH9 1TT).

Detail of the grave of Helen Bannerman, Grange Cemetery *Map p128* **P20**.

~ JAMES BOSWELL ~

1740–95, WRITER

James Boswell was born at Blair's Land, **Parliament Square** *Map p124* **Q13** (east side of St Giles Cathedral, Royal Mile, since demolished, EH1 1RE), the eldest son of a judge, Alexander Boswell, Lord Auchinleck, and his wife Euphemia Erskine. He attended the **Royal High School** *Map p126* **S14** (High School Yards, bottom of Infirmary Street, now the Archaeology Building of the University of Edinburgh, EH1 1LZ) then went to the **University of Edinburgh** *Map p126* **R14** (Old College, University of Edinburgh, South Bridge, plaque on north-west of quad, EH8 9YL) at the age of thirteen.

As a young man, he tried out different ideas about who he might become: he thought of converting to Catholicism and becoming a monk, and he determined to become an army officer. But when in London in the early 1760s, he met Samuel Johnson and many other notable people and discovered how much he enjoyed the company of women. This period also saw a grand tour of Europe and his meeting with Voltaire and Rousseau, before he returned to Edinburgh in 1766 and started his rather unsuccessful law practice, which carried on for the next seventeen years. He married his cousin Margaret Montgomerie in 1769.

In the 1770s, he and his wife rented a flat from David Hume, q.v., on the fourth floor of **James' Court** *Map p124* **P13** (493 Lawnmarket, Royal Mile, destroyed by fire in 1857, plaque at mid-entry, third storey of the western block, EH1 2PB) where he entertained Samuel Johnson, who was staying at the **White Horse Inn** *Map p126* **S13** (since demolished, Boyd's Entry, off St Mary's Street, carved plaque north side near corner, EH1 1SG). 'Mr Johnson and I walked arm-in-arm up the High Street... It was a dusky night; I could not prevent his being assailed by the evening effluvia of Edinburgh.' They also possibly dined at **Boswell's Court** *Map p124* **O13** (352 Castlehill, Royal Mile, EH1 2NF).

Boswell's Court, Castlehill, Royal Mile *Map p124* **O13**.

Boswell wrote *Tour of the Hebrides*, 1786, and the *Life of Samuel Johnson*, 1791, for which he won literary acclaim, with the latter praised as the best biography ever written. He also wrote a diary from the age of eighteen, which lay undiscovered for decades, and then was thought too racy to be published until the mid-twentieth century, because of mention of his erotic adventures. His friend David Hume described him as 'very good-humoured, very agreeable and very mad'. He died in London and was buried at Auchinleck, Ayrshire, the family seat. His portrait is in the **Scottish National Portrait Gallery** *Map p122* **P10** (1 Queen Street, gallery 5, second floor, EH2 1JD).

~ ROBERT BURNS ~

1759–96, POET

Robert Burness was born in Alloway, Ayrshire. He changed the spelling to Burns in 1786 upon the publication of his first collection of poetry, *Poems, Chiefly in the Scottish Dialect*, in Kilmarnock, which was a great success. He also worked variously as a surveyor, farmer and tax collector and even planned to go to Jamaica, where he had an offer to become a plantation overseer.

Burns set out for Edinburgh on a borrowed horse in 1786, looking for a publisher. At first he shared rooms with a friend in **Baxter's Close** *Map p124* **P13** (since demolished, first floor, 475 Lawnmarket, Royal Mile, now part of Lady Stair's Close, plaque above entrance to Lady Stair's Close, EH1 2PA), below a brothel. From there he went to the attic of another friend, William Nicol, in **Buccleuch Street** *Map p126* **R16** (since demolished, near 32 St Patrick's Square, EH8 9EU). After a trip in the country, he returned to live with a third friend, William Cruickshank, at **2 St James Square** *Map p122* **Q11** (south-west corner, since demolished, now site of St James Shopping Centre, Leith Street, EH1 3SS) when he was housebound following an injury to his leg. During this time he corresponded with Clarinda, q.v., a woman he became infatuated with but had met only twice.

He was successful in finding a publisher, William Smellie, who also introduced him to the Crochallan Fencibles, a drinking club that met in a tavern in **Anchor Close** *Map p124* **Q13** (off 243 High Street, Royal Mile, EH1 1PN and plaque, west wall of City Chambers, 253 High Street, Royal Mile, EH1 1YJ). He wrote bawdy songs for their amusement. He met the youthful Walter Scott, q.v., during the winter of 1786–87 at **Sciennes Hill House** *Map p128* **S18** (Sciennes House Place, off Causewayside, plaque north side, high to the left of no.5, EH9 1NN). On his last visit to Edinburgh in 1791, Burns stayed at the **White Hart Inn** *Map p124* **O14** (34 Grassmarket, plaque above and to the left of the door, EH1 2JU).

Burns is considered to have invented romantic poetry, but he was also a radical and an advocate for the common person, with his hope 'that man to man the world o'er shall brothers be for a' that'. He collected Scottish songs as well, which he sometimes expanded and revised. His wife, Jean Armour, bore him nine children, and he also fathered three others. Regarded as Scotland's national poet, he is commemorated at the **Writers' Museum** *Map p124* **P13** (Lady Stair's Close, Lawnmarket, off Royal Mile, portraits and artefacts, EH1 2PA), the **Scottish National Portrait Gallery** *Map p122* **P10** (1 Queen Street, gallery 7, second floor, also statue in entrance hall, EH2 1JD), the **Burns Monument** *Map p118* **T11** (7 Regent Road, EH8 8DP) and the **National Museum of Scotland** *Map p124* **Q14** (Chambers Street, 'Scotland Transformed', level 3, artefacts, EH1 1JF).

Robert Burns's cordial glass, Writers' Museum *Map p124* **P13**.

～ Thomas Carlyle ～

1795–1881, WRITER AND LITERARY CRITIC

Thomas Carlyle was born at Ecclefechan, Dumfriesshire, the son of a stonemason. At the age of fourteen, he walked the 100 miles to Edinburgh to begin his studies in theology at the university. After a few years, he left to be a mathematics teacher, only to return there in 1819, when he lived at **Simon Square** Map p126 **S15** (since demolished, EH8 9HP), where he suffered a crisis of faith. He went to live in **Moray Street** Map p118 **T7** (now Spey Street, EH7 4PY), near **Leith Walk** Map p118 **T7** (EH7 4PD), which is where he was when he realized that God did not exist. His first major work, *Sartor Resartus* (The Tailor Restored) used Leith Walk as the model for the fictional Rue St Thomas de l'Enfer. It was intended to be both factual and fictional, a new concept which was ahead of its time.

When in 1826 Carlyle married Jane Welsh, herself a writer, they went to live at **21 Comely Bank** Map p116 **I8** (plaque, EH4 1AL). Although 9,000 letters between them survive, the marriage was not always happy. Their friend, Samuel Butler, said, 'It was very good of God to let Carlyle and Mrs Carlyle marry one another, and so make only two people miserable and not four.'

In his historical writings, he postulated that history was shaped by dynamic individuals, or heroes, with biographies of Oliver Cromwell and Frederick the Great and an essay on Mohammed as examples. He wrote with intensity in his three-volume work, *The French Revolution, a History*, which brought him critical success. Now living in London, his work was influential on authors such as Charles Dickens, who used the book as a factual source for *A Tale of Two Cities*. His contributions to literary magazines such as the *Edinburgh Review* could be satirical and were often controversial, especially his social commentary.

In 1865 Carlyle was appointed rector of the **University of Edinburgh** Map p124 **Q16** (22a Buccleuch Place, plaque, EH8 9LN), an honour he said was the greatest of his life. A photo is in the **Scottish National Portrait Gallery** Map p122 **P10** (1 Queen Street, Photography Gallery, first floor, not always on display, EH2 1JD).

SIR ARTHUR CONAN DOYLE

1859–1930, WRITER

Arthur Ignatius Conan Doyle was born at **11 Picardy Place** *Map p118* **R9** (since demolished, plaque at 2 Picardy Place, and statue of Sherlock Holmes, EH1 3JT), the eldest of seven children of an Edinburgh family of Irish descent. His father, a civil servant, would later die in a mental institution. When he was sent to **Newington Academy** *Map p128* **S19** (since demolished, near 8 Salisbury Place, EH9 1SH), he lived at the home of a family friend at **Liberton Bank House** (off map, now Dunedin School, 1 Gilmerton Road, EH16 5TH), and then back with his family at **3 Sciennes Hill Place** *Map p128* **S18** (EH9 1NP). When he was later sent to boarding school in England, he would charge fees in food to other boys for telling them stories. In 1876 he started at **Edinburgh Medical School** *Map p124* **Q15** (University of Edinburgh, Old Medical School, Teviot Place, plaque within archway on left, EH8 9AG), lodging at **23 George Square** *Map p124* **Q16** (plaque, EH8 9LD). His tutor, Dr Joseph Bell, q.v., would become the model for Sherlock Holmes. He also came across the work of W. C. Honeyman, who had been 'inspired' by the accounts of James McLevy, q.v., a policeman who wrote about the Edinburgh underworld and how he solved crimes.

He started to write and publish short stories as a student. When he graduated and set up his medical practice in Plymouth and then in Southsea, few patients arrived, so he turned to writing. His first Sherlock Holmes story, *A Study in Scarlet*, was published in 1887. He wrote more of them for eighteen months, before deciding to kill off Holmes so that he could work on more serious historical subjects. However, he was forced to revive the detective after a public outcry.

Besides being a hugely successful author, he became an advisor to the police on criminal cases and devised useful forensic techniques. He also fought against miscarriages of justice, freeing the wrongly imprisoned. He took up other causes, including women's rights and inter-racial marriage, and supported new ideas, such as a Channel tunnel. But he is best remembered for the four novels and fifty-six short stories featuring the world's greatest detective, who never actually said, 'Elementary, my dear Watson'. He is commemorated at the **Surgeons' Hall Museum** *Map p126* **R14** (18 Nicolson Street, letter, EH8 9DW).

May 4th '92.

12, TENNISON ROAD,
SOUTH NORWOOD.

My dear Mr Bell –
Many thanks for your most kind and genial letter which was a very great pleasure to me. It is most certainly to you that I owe Sherlock Holmes, and though in the stories I have the advantage of being able to place him in all sorts of dramatic positions I do not think that his analytical work is in the least an exaggeration of some effects which I have seen you produce in the out-patient ward. Round the centre of deduction and inference and observation which I have heard you inculcate I have tried to build up a man who pushed the thing as far as it would go – further occasionally – and I am so glad

A letter from Conan Doyle to Dr Joseph Bell, Surgeons' Hall Museum *Map p126* **R14.**

∽ DOROTHY DUNNETT ∽

1923–2001, WRITER AND PAINTER

Dorothy Halliday was born in Dunfermline. The family moved to **13 Craigs Avenue** (off map, EH12 8HS) when she was ten. She attended **James Gillespie's High School for Girls** Map p128 **N18** (22–32 Warrender Park Crescent, now university student residences, EH9 1DY), immortalized by Muriel Spark, q.v., and then went on to **Edinburgh College of Art** Map p124 **O15** (74 Lauriston Place, EH3 9DF) and Glasgow School of Art. Her first job was as a press officer in the Scottish civil service. When she married the journalist Alastair Dunnett at **Corstorphine Old Parish Church** (off map, 2a Corstorphine High Street, EH12 7ST) they moved to **87 Colinton Road** Map p128 **I22** (EH10 5DF), where she lived until her death.

She wrote her first novel, *The Game of Kings*, at the suggestion of her husband after she had complained of having nothing to read. It was turned down by five British publishers, before the American firm, Putnam, agreed to take it. Published in 1961 it became part of the *Lymond Chronicles*, eventually six novels, set in mid-sixteenth-century Europe, detailing the life of a Scottish nobleman, Francis Crawford of Lymond, a romantic hero modelled on her husband. More historical fiction followed, with an eight-part prequel, *The House of Niccolò*, which tells the story of Lymond's ancestors. Dunnett prided herself on her meticulous research in her tales of suspense and action.

While Dunnett is best known for historical fiction, she also wrote a novel about the real Macbeth, *King Hereafter*, and a series of mystery novels about a portrait painter who was also a spy. An accomplished painter herself, she exhibited frequently at the **Royal Scottish Academy** Map p122 **O12** (The Mound, EH2 2EL) and had portraits commissioned by prominent figures, including members of the judiciary and Lord Thomson of Fleet, q.v.

The Dorothy Dunnett Society keeps her memory alive and holds annual gatherings at the **Royal Over-Seas League** Map p122 **N12** (100 Princes Street, EH2 3AB). She is also commemorated with a memorial stone in the Makars' Court of the **Writers' Museum** Map p124 **P13** (Lady Stair's Close, Lawnmarket, off Royal Mile, EH1 2PA). A renaissance woman, her reputation rests primarily on her historical romances, with their complex plots and dashing heroes, all helping to make history accessible to her many readers.

The stone with Dorothy Dunnett's words at the Makars' Court of the Writers' Museum
Map p124 **P13**.

~ ROBERT FERGUSSON ~

1750–74, POET

Robert Fergusson was born in **Cap and Feather Close** *Map p126* **R13** (since demolished, near Niddry Street, EH1 1LG), the son of a haberdasher's clerk. In 1764 he went to St Andrews University to study divinity but had to abandon his studies when his father died. To support his family at **Jamieson's Land** *Map p126* **R13** (since demolished, near corner of Cowgate and Blackfriars Street, EH1 1NE) he became a clerk in the Commissionary Office, copying wills and matrimonial documents. He wrote poetry in his free time, often about the ordinary people of Edinburgh. He joined the Cape Club, a convivial literary society, which met in **Craig's Close** *Map p124* **Q13** (middle of south side of Cockburn Street, plaque, EH1 1BN). At first he wrote in standard English, but in 1772 he turned to vernacular Scots. Nearly all of his poetry was written between 1771 and 1773.

His portrayals of street life were composed with humour and based on keen observation. Whether of goings-on in taverns or at the races, they are fresh and evocative, all conveyed with affection for those depicted. Poems such as *Callers Oysters* and *Auld Reekie* are considered among his best, inspired by the work of Allan Ramsay, q.v., and the Latin poets. His first collection was published in 1773, with 500 copies sold, earning him £50.

By 1774, he was suffering from depression, possibly exacerbated by a serious fall, and was sent to **Bedlam** *Map p124* **Q15** (since demolished, now Napier's, 18 Bristo Place, EH1 1EZ), a damp and unheated mental institution, where he soon died at the age of twenty-four. He was buried in a pauper's grave at the **Canongate Kirk** *Map p118* **T12** (153 Canongate, middle west side of church, EH8 8BN). Thirteen years later, Robert Burns, q.v., paid for a headstone for his unmarked grave. There is now also a life-size sculpture of him outside the **Canongate Kirk** *Map p118* **T12** (sculpture by David Annand, 153 Canongate, EH8 8BN), he is commemorated in **St Giles Cathedral** *Map p124* **Q13** (Royal Mile, south aisle, EH1 1RE), and a lock of his hair is in the **Writers' Museum** *Map p124* **P13** (Lady Stair's Close, Lawnmarket, off Royal Mile, EH1 2PA).

Also admired by Robert Louis Stevenson, q.v., Fergusson inspired Scots to write in the vernacular and to concentrate on life as they saw it. He has been called Edinburgh's greatest poet.

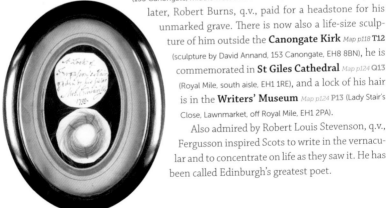

Lock of Robert Fergusson's hair, Writers' Museum *Map p124* **P13**.

⟋ NORMAN MacCAIG ⟍

1910–96, POET

Norman Alexander McCaig was born at **53 East London Street** *Map p116* Q8 (EH7 4BW). The family later lived at **11 Dundas Street** *Map p122* O10 (EH3 6QG), when his father's chemist's shop was below at number 9. He studied at the Royal High School and the University of Edinburgh, then trained at **Moray House College of Education** *Map p126* S13 (St John Street, off Royal Mile, now part of the University of Edinburgh, EH8 8AQ) and spent his working life as a primary school teacher and headmaster, latterly at **Kings Inch School** (off map, since demolished, now Inch View Care Home, 233 Gilmerton Road, EH16 5UD). As an adult, he changed the spelling of his surname to MacCaig.

MacCaig's first collection of poetry was published in 1943, and he then wrote prolifically throughout his life. Much of his subject matter concerned Edinburgh and Assynt in the western Highlands of Scotland, where he had a second home. His Edinburgh poetry could be about tenement life or its violent past. He frequently gave readings in Edinburgh and elsewhere, much appreciated by his audience. His lucid, anti-cerebral and accessible poetry was always written in English, to the dismay of some, who felt it was important to use Scots or Gaelic. Fond of conversation and the company of other poets, he enjoyed meeting them in favourite haunts, such as the **Southern Bar** *Map p128* S17 (22–26 South Clerk Street, EH8 9PR) and **Milnes Bar** *Map p122* O11 (35 Hanover Street, EH2 2PJ).

During World War II, MacCaig was a conscientious objector and was imprisoned for a time. In 1967 he gave up teaching and became the **University of Edinburgh's** *Map p126* R16 (Department of English Literature, David Hume Tower, George Square, EH8 9JX) first Fellow in Creative Writing. A modest man, he was also known for his wit, once describing his religion as Zen Calvinism. In his latter years, he received several honours and was considered the grand old man of Scottish poetry. From 1943 until his death he lived at **7 Leamington Terrace** *Map p128* L17 (EH10 4JW). A sculpture is at **Lochside Walkway** (off map, near Lochside Avenue, South Gyle, sculpture, north-east of lochs, EH12 9DJ), a group portrait with other poets in the **Scottish National Portrait Gallery** *Map p122* P10 (1 Queen Street, gallery 11, first floor, 'Poets' Pub', EH2 1JD), and an example of his poetry is carved on the side of the **Scottish Parliament** building *Map p118* U12 (Horse Wynd, poem on side of building in Canongate, EH99 1SP).

Norman MacCaig's poem on the side of the Scottish Parliament building, Canongate *Map p118* U12.

ALEXANDER McCALL SMITH

1948–, WRITER

Alexander McCall Smith was born in southern Rhodesia, now Zimbabwe. He studied law at the University of Edinburgh, where he obtained a PhD in the subject. He taught in Belfast, at the same time writing both children's stories and academic texts, before returning to Africa in 1981, where he co-founded the law school at the University of Botswana. In 1984 he returned to Edinburgh, eventually becoming professor of medical law.

He first came to public attention with his novel, *The No. 1 Ladies' Detective Agency*, in 1999. Set in Botswana, it became the first in a series of fourteen, and was a huge success from the start, with millions sold. The emphasis was on small incidents and the personalities of the main characters, all portrayed with humour and a lightness of touch. McCall Smith went on to create two other series set in Edinburgh, *44 Scotland Street* and *The Sunday Philosophy Club*, which gently mock the foibles of middle-class Edinburgh.

The nearest address to the fictional 44 Scotland Street is **39 Scotland Street** *Map p116* **P8** (EH3 6PY). Many other real locations are mentioned in the series, which was written in episodes for *The Scotsman* newspaper. Characters visit the **Glass & Thompson café** *Map p122* **O10** (2 Dundas Street, EH3 6HZ) or do their food shopping at **Valvona & Crolla** *Map p118* **S9** (19 Elm Row, EH7 4AA), while the more well-heeled head for **Jenner's Department Store** *Map p122* **P12** (48 Princes Street, café on fifth floor, EH2 2YJ). Real people also figure. The artist Elizabeth Blackadder, q.v., and the director of the Scottish Gallery, Guy Peploe, grandson of and authority on Samuel Peploe, q.v., are among those who have roles. The main character in the *Sunday Philosophy Club*, Isabel Dalhousie, lives in Merchiston, as do McCall Smith and his family.

McCall Smith has received many honours, both for his best-selling books and as an international authority on the law of bioethics. His books have been translated into forty-four languages. An amateur bassoonist, he is also the co-founder of the Really Terrible Orchestra. His bust is in the **Scottish National Portrait Gallery** *Map p122* **P10** (1 Queen Street, bust on west stair, between first and second floors, EH2 1JD).

Glass & Thompson café, Dundas Street *Map p122* **O10**.

SIR COMPTON MACKENZIE

1883–1972, WRITER

Edward Montague Compton Mackenzie, always known as Monty, was born in West Hartlepool. His parents were touring actors passing through, and they continued to be on the move through his early childhood. Once they settled in London, he excelled at school and went on to Magdalen College, Oxford, where he decided to become a poet. He secretly married an actress in 1905. His father, now a successful theatre manager, backed the tour of his first play. At the **Royal Lyceum Theatre** *Map p124* **M14** (30b Grindlay Street, EH3 9AX), in 1907, Mackenzie had the lead role and was applauded as both actor and author.

After mixed reviews for his poetry, he turned to writing novels, eventually with over a hundred to his name, and was an immediate success, both critical and popular. However, both he and his wife were always extravagant and had many financial crises. During World War I, he was in counter-espionage in Athens, but when he later wrote about it he was prosecuted and the books withdrawn.

After living in Capri and the Channel Islands, he went to Barra in the Hebrides. He was head of the Home Guard during World War II when the SS *Politician* ran aground with a huge cargo of whisky. The event became the basis of his comic novel *Whisky Galore!*, later a film. *Monarch of the Glen*, a gentle mockery of Highland personalities, became a television series and assured his continuing fame.

He moved to **31 Drummond Place** *Map p122* **P9** (carved in stone, right of door, EH3 6PW) in 1953 with his secretary, who became his wife in 1962. Her sister ran a hairdresser's salon from the premises, and she became his third wife when her sister died. He lived there until his death.

A man of passion, he was a co-founder of the forerunner of the Scottish National Party and a member of the Campaign for Nuclear Disarmament. His portrait is in the **Scottish National Portrait Gallery** *Map p122* **P10** (1 Queen Street, gallery 11, first floor, EH2 1JD), and a film poster is in the **National Museum of Scotland** *Map p124* **Q14** (Chambers Street, 'Scotland, a Changing Nation', level 6, north-west section, EH1 1JF).

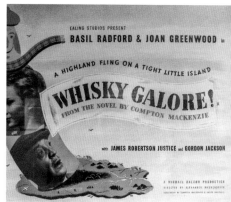

Poster for the 1949 film *Whisky Galore!*, National Museum of Scotland *Map p124* **Q14**.

~ Thomas de Quincey ~

1785–1859, WRITER

Thomas de Quincey was born in Manchester. After grammar school, he ran away to Wales, living on the goodwill of various people, before going to London, where he was equally penniless. This period of deprivation was a strong influence on his later writing. He reconnected with his family, who sent him to Oxford in 1804, where he first took opium for toothache. He would continue to take it on and off for the rest of his life. The taking of opiates was not then illegal and was viewed more as a shortcoming than a health risk.

De Quincey admired the poetry of Wordsworth and Coleridge and so set off to the Lake District to meet them in 1809. Once acquainted, he settled there for ten years. He tried to cut down his consumption of opium, felt better and married the eighteen-year-old daughter of a farmer. His most celebrated work, *Confessions of an English Opium-Eater*, was published in 1822, and he became well-known, meeting other authors and writing prolifically for important literary magazines, including the *Edinburgh Review* and *Blackwood's Magazine*. Despite working constantly, between his drug habit, his generosity and his desire to collect books, he was constantly in debt.

WRITERS

Moving to Edinburgh at this time, he lived at many addresses, including **9 Great King Street** Map p122 **O9** (EH3 6QW), **1 Forres Street** Map p120 **L11** (EH3 6BJ) and **29 Ann Street** Map p120 **K10** (EH4 1PL), lodging at the last with the author Christopher North. Still financially insecure, he would sometimes take refuge in the Royal Sanctuary of Holyrood at **Abbey Strand** Map p118 **U12** (EH8 8DX). In this debtors' sanctuary he was safe from creditors but had the freedom to leave on Sundays, when he would visit his friends and enjoy their conviviality. Known as a conversationalist, he is credited with coining 159 words, including subconscious and intuit. Among the many authors he influenced are Edgar Allan Poe and Charles Baudelaire. He died at **42 Lothian Street** Map p124 **Q15** (since demolished, near Potterrow Student Centre, University of Edinburgh, 5/2 Bristo Square, EH8 9AL) and is buried at **St Cuthbert's Church** Map p124 **M13** (5 Lothian Road, down Lothian Road steps, first path on right, round curve, sharp left, then seventh monument in right-hand wall, EH1 2EP).

Abbey Strand, part of the Royal Sanctuary of Holyrood, where debtors such as Thomas de Quincey were beyond the reach of the law Map p118 **U12**.

⌁ ALLAN RAMSAY THE ELDER ⌁

1686–1758, POET

Born in Lanarkshire, Allan Ramsay's father died soon after his birth and he was sent at fourteen to Edinburgh as an apprentice to a Grassmarket wigmaker. When he became a wigmaker in his own right, he set up in business at **155 High Street** Map p126 **R13** (since demolished, near 137 High Street, Royal Mile, near north-east corner of North Bridge, EH1 1SG). However, he preferred to write poetry, and in 1712 he was one of the founders of the Easy Club, for young men interested in literature and politics, where he began to read his poetry aloud. Their encouragement meant that he began to publish and sell his own and others' work by 1718 from his premises. Well-known works include *Tea Table Miscellany*, a collection of Scots songs and ballads, and what is considered his best work, *The Gentle Shepherd*, a play published in 1725.

WRITERS

His success was such that he was able to become a full-time bookseller in new premises at the **Luckenbooths** Map p124 **Q13** (since demolished, middle of the Royal Mile near St Giles Cathedral, first floor, east end, EH1 1RE), which was so popular, it was nicknamed the Hub of the Universe. There he opened the first lending library in Scotland, with the latest works from London. These scandalous books caused a raid by magistrates in 1728, but he persisted. In 1736 he provoked further outrage when he opened a theatre in **Carrubber's Close** Map p126 **R13** (135 High Street, off the Royal Mile, EH1 1SJ). It was shut by magistrates the following year, and theatres in Edinburgh were not licensed until six years after his death.

He wrote little after 1726 and retired about 1740 to **Ramsay Lodge** Map p124 **O13** (Ramsay Gardens, EH1 2NA), the octagonal house he had built. He is buried in **Greyfriars Kirkyard** Map p124 **P14** (1 Greyfriars Place, plaque high on south outer wall of church near back, EH1 2QQ). His statue is in **West Princes Street Gardens** Map p122 **O12** (south-west corner of the Mound and Princes Street, EH2 4BJ), and his portrait and bust in the **Scottish National Portrait Gallery** Map p122 **P10** (1 Queen Street, gallery 5, second floor, EH2 1JD).

In his poetry, he revived interest in the vernacular tradition and celebrated Edinburgh's lowliest people. A poet, satirist and songwriter, he wrote in both Scots and English. He is credited with inspiring Robert Fergusson, q.v., and Robert Burns, q.v., and has been called the best pastoral writer ever.

Ramsay Lodge, the octagonal building with the pointed roof known as the goose-pie house Map p124 **O13**.

⁓ Ian Rankin ⁓

1960–, WRITER

Ian Rankin was born in Fife and graduated from the University of Edinburgh, before going to London and France to write, supporting himself doing a myriad of low-paid jobs. He returned to the university to do a PhD, but his thesis on Muriel Spark, q.v., remained uncompleted. During this time he began to write novels, the first of which was published in 1987. He created the enduring character Detective Inspector John Rebus, who was to be the protagonist of seventeen dark crime novels. The award-winning thrillers sell 100,000 copies per title and are set mainly in Edinburgh, using actual locations. Many have been adapted for television, with John Hannah and later Ken Stott, q.v., as Rebus.

Rankin lived opposite and stared out of the window at **24 Arden Street** Map p128 **O19** (EH9 1BW) while writing his first published book, *Knots and Crosses*, so it became the home of DI Rebus. Rebus's girlfriend, Patience Aitken, lives in the more upmarket **Oxford Terrace** Map p120 **J10** (EH4 1PX). Rebus works at **St Leonards Police Station** Map p126 **T16** (14 St Leonard's Street, EH8 9QW) and drinks at the **Oxford Bar** Map p122 **M11** (8 Young Street, EH2 4JB), which Rankin also enjoys.

In his 2001 story, *The Falls*, a central clue is a doll in a miniature coffin, which Rebus connects to the mysterious Arthur's Seat coffins, seventeen wooden figures in miniature coffins that were discovered in a cave in 1836, in the **National Museum of Scotland** Map p124 **Q14** (Chambers Street, 'Scotland, a Changing Nation', level 6, north-west section, miniature coffins and Rankin papers, EH1 1JF). Their purpose is unknown, whether malevolent, protective or commemorative. In *Set in Darkness*, the body of a prospective MP is found at the soon-to-be-opened **Scottish Parliament** Map p118 **U12** (Horse Wynd, EH99 1SP). And in *Strip Jack*, a woman's body is found in the Water of Leith under the **Dean Bridge** Map p120 **K11** (Queensferry Road, EH4 3AS). Rankin used the name of **Fleshmarket Close** Map p124 **Q13** (199 High Street, off the Royal Mile, EH1 1QA) in his eponymous novel of 2004 to make the connection with human trafficking, the sale of people's lives.

Rankin has connected himself to Edinburgh's literary past and has never wanted to be seen as a genre writer. Besides the best-selling Rebus books, he has written graphic novels, short stories and a television documentary. He lives with his family in the Merchiston area of Edinburgh known as Writers' Block.

The Arthur's Seat coffins, 1836, at the National Museum of Scotland Map p124 **Q14**.

WRITERS

⌒ J. K. ROWLING ⌒

1965–, WRITER

Joanne Rowling, pronounced 'rolling', was born near Bristol. She studied at the University of Exeter, then went to Portugal to teach English. She married a Portuguese journalist and had a daughter, but when the marriage failed in 1993, she came to Edinburgh to be near her younger sister, who lived at **140 Marchmont Road** *Map p128* **P20** (EH9 1AQ). Rowling lived first at **28 Gardner's Crescent** *Map p120* **L15** (EH3 8DF), before moving to **7 South Lorne Place, Leith** *Map p118* **V6** (EH6 8QN).

As a single mother, she lived on benefit and would take her daughter to cafés while she wrote her first Harry Potter novel, which she had conceived and started writing in 1990. Her favourites were **Nicolson's Café** *Map p126* **R14** (now the Spoon Café Bistro, first floor, 6a Nicolson Street, EH8 9DH), owned by her brother-in-law, and the **Elephant House** *Map p124* **P14** (21 George IV Bridge, EH1 1EN). She did a teaching degree at Moray House College of Education, taking placements at St David's Roman Catholic High School in Dalkeith and at nearby Leith Academy. *Harry Potter and the Philosopher's Stone* was completed in 1995 and initially rejected by twelve publishers. However, Bloomsbury published it in 1997, but in an edition of only 1,000. When it won several awards, the American rights were sold for more than $100,000. Now wealthy, Rowling gave up teaching and moved to **19 Hazelbank Terrace** *Map p128* **F21** (EH11 1SL). She acquired her middle initial from her grandmother's name, Kathleen, and used her initials, since the publishers thought boys wouldn't read a book by a woman.

The seven fantasy books follow the boy wizard through his school career. The series has sold towards half a billion copies and been turned into eight films, making Rowling among the wealthiest women in Britain. Spin-offs range from toys to a Harry Potter theme park. She gives substantial amounts to and is active in several charities. She now writes books for both adults and children. Copies of her books are in the **National Museum of Scotland** *Map p124* **Q14** (Chambers Street, 'Scotland, a Changing Nation', level 6, north-west section, signed presentation box, EH1 1JF). She lives with her family in the Merchiston area of Edinburgh known as Writers' Block.

The interior of the Elephant House, where J. K. Rowling wrote her first Harry Potter book *Map p124* **P14**.

~ SIR WALTER SCOTT ~

1771–1832, WRITER AND POET

Walter Scott was born in **College Wynd** *Map p124* **Q14** (now Guthrie Street, since demolished, carved in stone at first-floor level, east side near corner of Chambers Street, EH1 1HR), the son of a solicitor and the ninth of twelve children, six of whom died in infancy. At eighteen months, he contracted polio, leaving him lame in the right leg. Educated at the University of Edinburgh from the age of twelve, he qualified as a lawyer in 1792. Between 1774 and 1797 the family lived at **25 George Square** *Map p124* **Q16** (plaque, EH8 9LD). After he married Margaret Charlotte Charpenter in 1797, the couple went to live at **39 North Castle Street** *Map p122* **M11** (carved in stone, above middle window, EH2 3BG) for twenty-eight years.

His series of romantic narrative poems including *The Lady of the Lake* were both critical and commercial successes. Feeling overshadowed by Byron, however, he turned to historical novels set in Scotland, at first writing anonymously as novels were not a respectable form. His heroic creations include Rob Roy and Ivanhoe, both to become popular films. Well-known novels are *The Heart of Midlothian*, *Waverley* and *The Antiquary*. Influenced by the eighteenth-century Enlightenment, Scott wrote about tolerance and the value of every human being, regardless of social rank. As the inventor of historical fiction, he became one of Europe's most famous literary figures. He was created a baronet in 1818, and when George IV visited Scotland in 1822, Scott acted as a sort of stage manager, emphasizing the tartan and romantic Highland image of Scotland. His good nature, generosity and modesty, coupled with his enjoyment of large-scale entertaining, made him a popular figure.

In 1823 he co-founded the **Edinburgh Academy** *Map p116* **M8** (42 Henderson Row, EH3 5BL), but his partnership in a failed publishing house caused financial disaster. He spent the rest of his life writing furiously to save himself from bankruptcy. The **Scott Monument** *Map p122* **P12** (East Princes Street Gardens, EH2 2EJ), erected in 1844, shows the enormous status he enjoyed in Victorian Britain. Artefacts can be seen at the **Writers' Museum** *Map p124* **P13** (Lady Stair's Close, Lawnmarket, off Royal Mile, portraits and artefacts, EH1 2PA) and the **National Museum of Scotland** *Map p124* **Q14** (Chambers Street, level 5, south, EH1 1JF), and his portrait and bust are in the **Scottish National Portrait Gallery** *Map p122* **P10** (1 Queen Street, gallery 7, second floor, EH2 1JD).

Half-hour glass, National Museum of Scotland, which Walter Scott used to pace his writing *Map p124* **Q14**.

MURIEL SPARK
1918–2006, WRITER

Muriel Sarah Camberg was born and brought up in Bruntsfield and would walk over the **Bruntsfield Links** *Map p128* **M18** (interpretation board in park near Bruntsfield Place, EH9 9EX) to the nearby **James Gillespie's High School for Girls** *Map p128* **N18** (22–32 Warrender Park Crescent, now university student residences, EH9 1DY). It was to become the model for the Marcia Blaine School for Girls in her 1961 novel, *The Prime of Miss Jean Brodie*, the book which became a television series, play and film and was to make her a household name and financially secure. One of the locations used in the 1969 film was the gates of the **Edinburgh Academy** *Map p116* **M8** (gates left of main entrance, with added over-gate in the film, 54 Henderson Row, EH3 5BL).

Her family were working-class, her father Jewish and her mother part-Jewish. After school, she went to **Heriot-Watt College** *Map p124* **Q14** (now Crown Office, 23–25 Chambers Street, EH1 1LA) where her course in précis writing helped to form her economical authorial voice. She then taught at a private primary school, the **Hill School** *Map p128* **K21** (now private home, 35 Colinton Road, EH10 5EN), and later worked in the offices of **Small's Department Store** *Map p122* **N12** (William Small and Sons, now shoe shop, 106 Princes Street, EH2 3AA).

She married Sydney Spark in 1937 and went to southern Rhodesia, now Zimbabwe, with him. She had a son, but characterized the marriage as disastrous and left for London in 1940, where she worked for British Intelligence, inventing news stories 'to discredit the enemy'.

She worked incessantly at her writing, and a turning point came when she won a short story prize run by the *Observer* in 1951, coming first out of 6,700 entries. An attractive, well-dressed woman, she was now much in demand. She converted to Catholicism in 1954, which she considered crucial to the development of her writing. Apparently restless, she lived in New York sporadically in the early 1960s, eventually settling in Italy in 1967 where she lived until her death.

Spark was twice shortlisted for the Booker Prize, was awarded many other honours and was created a Dame of the British Empire in 1993. Her prolific output included poetry, biographies, short stories and novels. Her portrait is in the café of the **Scottish National Portrait Gallery** *Map p122* **P10** (1 Queen Street, EH2 1JD).

The gates at the Edinburgh Academy, used with an added over-gate in the film of *The Prime of Miss Jean Brodie* to represent the entrance to the Marcia Blaine School for Girls *Map p116* **M8**.

～ ROBERT LOUIS STEVENSON ～

1850–94, WRITER

Born Robert Lewis Balfour Stevenson, an only child, at **8 Howard Place** *Map p116* **N7** (plaque, EH3 5JZ), the family settled at **17 Heriot Row** *Map p122* **N10** (carved in stone, brass plaque with poem, EH3 6HP) between 1857 and 1880, opposite the Queen Street Gardens, where his nurse, Alison Cunningham, would take him to play. His father was a lighthouse engineer, as were several family members. Often too ill to go to school throughout his childhood, he would still go ice-skating at **Canonmills Loch** *Map p116* **O8** (now drained, King George V Park, Eyre Place, EH3 5EN) or walk along the Water of Leith.

He was determined to become a writer, but to placate his father he enrolled at the University of Edinburgh in engineering, then switched to law, qualifying as an advocate in 1875. However, he rarely attended classes, preferring to edit the university magazine and participate in a literary society, which would adjourn to **Rutherford's Bar** *Map p126* **R14** (now the Hispaniola, 3 Drummond Street, also plaque Drummond Street, north-east corner with South Bridge, EH8 9TT). Summers and 'winter retreats' were spent at **Swanston Cottage** (off map, 108 Swanston Road, EH10 7DS) for its fresh air and healthy food, between 1867 and 1880.

He went to France for his health in 1873 and met his future wife, Fanny Osbourne, at an artists' colony there in 1876. He wrote about his travels in France, Belgium and the USA, and in 1883 published *Treasure Island*. Other successes included *Kidnapped* and *The Strange Case of Dr Jekyll and Mr Hyde* in 1886, the latter inspired by Deacon Brodie, q.v. He became a celebrity in his own lifetime, although for much of the twentieth century he was regarded as merely a writer of children's and horror literature. Now rehabilitated, many authors have cited his influence, and he remains popular worldwide.

Still plagued by a lung condition, he and his wife moved to Samoa in 1890, where he lived until his death from a haemorrhage. He is commemorated with a birch grove memorial in **West Princes Street Gardens** *Map p124* **N13** (EH2 4BJ), in **St Giles Cathedral** *Map p124* **Q13** (Royal Mile, outer south aisle (Moray Aisle), west wall, EH1 1RE) at the **Writers' Museum** *Map p124* **P13** (Lady Stair's Close, Lawnmarket, off Royal Mile, many artefacts, EH1 2PA), at the **National Museum of Scotland** *Map p124* **Q14** (Chambers Street, 'Facing the Sea', level 3, dance skirt, EH1 1JF), and the family tomb is in **New Calton Burial Ground** *Map p118* **U11** (Regent Road, family tomb with gates, middle of east wall, EH8 8DR).

The dance skirt that was placed on Robert Louis Stevenson's grave in Samoa, National Museum of Scotland *Map p124* **Q14**.

WRITERS

⟋ IRVINE WELSH ⟍

1957–, WRITER

Irvine John Welsh was born at **13 Canonmills** Map p116 **O7** (since demolished, near petrol station, EH3 5HA). The family later lived in Leith, West Pilton and Muirhouse, all less salubrious parts of Edinburgh. He left **Ainslie Park High School** Map p116 **E3** (now north campus of Telford College, Crewe Road North, EH5 2NE) at sixteen and soon headed for London where he revelled in the punk scene and dabbled in petty crime. He returned to Edinburgh, first working in the city's housing department and then studying for an MBA at Heriot-Watt University, using his time in the **library** (off map, university library, second floor, Riccarton, EH14 4AS) to write both his thesis and his first novel, *Trainspotting*, published in 1993. In it he detailed the world of the underclass, the drugs culture and life on Edinburgh's housing estates, a subject never before tackled and all written in the language of the streets – angry, hard-bitten and indecipherable to many English speakers. It became a sensation, praised and damned in equal measure, and was turned into a play performed at the **Traverse Theatre** Map p124 **M14** (10 Cambridge Street, EH1 2ED) and a 1996 film.

'Trainspotting' is an ironic reference to the long-disused **Leith Central Railway Station** Map p118 **V4** (now derelict, corner of Leith Walk and Duke Street, EH6 8LN), where it is therefore impossible to see a train. Set mostly in Leith in the late 1980s, it chronicles the boredom and brutality of the lives of its central characters. Both Welsh's flat and the childhood home of the fictional Sick Boy were in **Cables Wynd House** Map p118 **U2** (Cables Wynd, EH6 6DQ), known as the Banana Block for its curved shape. Begbie's local was the **Central Bar** Map p118 **U4** (7–9 Leith Walk, EH6 8LN), while Welsh's favourite Leith pub was the **Boundary Bar** Map p118 **T7** (now City Limits Bar, 379 Leith Walk, EH6 8SE).

Now able to write full-time, Welsh went on to publish *Porno* in 2002, followed by five more novels and four collections of short stories. He is also the author of a 2007 television drama, *Wedding Belles*, filmed at the Banana Block.

Welsh now lives in Chicago, returning to Edinburgh occasionally to support Hibernian football club (Hibs). The poster for the film *Trainspotting* and the original script are in the **National Museum of Scotland** Map p124 **Q14** (Chambers Street, 'Scotland, a Changing Nation', level 6, north-west section, EH1 1JF).

The autographed copy of the film script of *Trainspotting*, National Museum of Scotland Map p124 **Q14**.

WRITERS

4

PIONEERS

Edinburgh was a centre of medical education from the eighteenth century, so it will come as no surprise that this section includes several pioneering doctors. The University of Edinburgh soon became so well known for its medical education that it attracted students from around the world. Joseph Lister is remembered for antisepsis, while James Simpson's discovery of the powers of chloroform allowed numerous people to have pain-free operations. Both were responsible for saving thousands of lives. You will find scientists in almost every field here as well, from vets to chemists. Education was always valued in Scotland, even when it allowed students to challenge prevailing opinion.

Because of the questioning attitude engendered by the Scottish Enlightenment of the late eighteenth century, pioneers were able to go beyond conventional wisdom and to consider the unthinkable. James Hutton conjectured that rock formations were due not to the biblical Flood, but to heat from the Earth's molten core. Adam Smith thought that morals had no connection to Christianity.

In more modern times, Alexander Graham Bell used his interest in audiology to create the beginning of an international system of telecommunications. Fifty years ago, Peter Higgs had theorized that a particle now called the Higgs boson by some and the God particle by others gives other particles their mass. Ground-breaking experiments at CERN seem to prove him correct, putting him in line for a Nobel prize.

In the fields of religion and philosophy, we also have the unlikely bedfellows of John Knox and David Hume. Knox was responsible for the type of Protestantism prevalent in Scotland, still influential today, much to the consternation of many. Hume, a sceptic, said that religious belief was not a rational process and was consequently charged with heresy.

Two women doctors, Elsie Inglis and Sophia Jex-Blake, had to fight prejudice just to be able to enrol at medical school and went on to fight for women's rights and in particular to have other women similarly educated. Joseph Bell and Henry Littlejohn pioneered forensic science, helping the police to find clues in previously overlooked material. The vet William Dick was more concerned with animals, founding one of the first veterinary colleges.

Much earlier, John Napier wrestled with mathematics and came up with calculating devices and logarithms. The chemist Joseph Black discovered carbon dioxide and its properties. James Clerk Maxwell is considered the father of electronics, with his work later allowing the development of radio, television and radar. Patrick Geddes was the father of a completely different field, town planning, arguing for a make-do-and-mend approach, rather than wholesale slum clearance.

The pioneers were free thinkers who often led unconventional lives, matching their lifestyles with their beliefs. They were definitely not pillars of the establishment, but had the courage of their convictions, even when the rest of the world disapproved of them.

The last resting place of John Knox, under space 23 in the car park south of St Giles Cathedral. You have the opportunity of paying your respects or dancing on his grave *Map p124* **Q13**.

～ Alexander Graham Bell ～

1847–1922, INVENTOR

Alexander Graham Bell was born at **16 South Charlotte Street** *Map p122* **M12** (carved in stone, left of door, EH2 4AX), the middle of three sons. His two brothers died of tuberculosis, and he was also sickly. His mother was hearing-impaired, and his father and other relatives worked on elocution and the mechanics of speech, leading to an early interest in sound. He was educated at the **Hamilton Place Academy** *Map p120* **L9** (10–11 Hamilton Place, now shop, EH3 5AU) and the **Royal High School** *Map p118* **T11** (Old Royal High School, 5–7 Regent Road, EH1 3DG), before going to London aged fifteen to learn about electricity, telegraphy and acoustics. Upon his return to Edinburgh in 1864, his father challenged him to create a speaking machine. He and his brother produced a mechanical head whose 'voice' was powered by bellows.

After study at the **University of Edinburgh** *Map p126* **R14** (Old College, South Bridge, EH8 9YL) and a short time in London, the family emigrated to Canada, seeking a more healthy climate. In 1871 he went to Boston to work at a school for the deaf. Bell then joined the many other inventors who were trying to develop a telephone, since telegraph lines had been in place for about thirty years. In 1876, at the age of twenty-nine, he was the first to create a practical, working model and patent it, now considered the most valuable patent ever. When he demonstrated the device to Queen Victoria, she pronounced it 'most extraordinary'.

He worked tirelessly and was responsible for many other inventions, especially in the field of sound, such as the phonograph and the audiometer for the detection of hearing problems, but also ranging from the hydrofoil to a metal detector. With collaborators he developed a motor-powered aeroplane, and in 1908 his *Silver Dart* made the first successful flight in Canada. He has been called one of the most influential people in human history.

Exhibits of early Bell telephones are in the **National Museum of Scotland** *Map p124* **Q14** (Chambers Street, 'Communicate!' level 3, and 'Shaping Our World' level 5, EH1 1JF) and his photograph is in the **Scottish National Portrait Gallery** *Map p122* **P10** (1 Queen Street, gallery 11, first floor, photo in drawer, EH2 1JD). But Bell said of his most famous invention, 'I never use the beast.'

Bell-patented telephones, National Museum of Scotland *Map p124* **Q14**.

～ Dr Joseph Bell ～

1837–1911, DOCTOR AND FORENSIC SCIENTIST

Joseph Bell was born at **22 St Andrew Square** *Map p122* **P11** (EH2 1BG), the eldest of nine children. He studied first at Leiden and then at the Edinburgh Medical School, becoming the third generation of his family to qualify as a doctor. He became the house surgeon at the Royal Infirmary as well as teaching students, one of whom was Arthur Conan Doyle, q.v., who also became his clerk.

While he was a respected surgeon, he was best known for his powers of diagnosis, both of illness and of occupation and character. His abilities made him one of the sources for the fictional character of Sherlock Holmes. At the Outpatients Clinic of the **Royal Infirmary** *Map p126* **R14** (now School of GeoSciences, University of Edinburgh, Drummond Street, EH8 9XP), he would make a diagnosis and challenge his students to work out his reasoning. He emphasized the importance of close observation by pointing out tiny details which most would have overlooked. His success was due to a combination of an analytical mind, intuition and his powers of observation.

With Sir Henry Littlejohn, q.v., he was a pioneer of forensic science, and both men were possibly brought in to try to solve the Jack the Ripper case in London, as well as dealing with more local ones, such as that of Jessie King, q.v. He served as Queen Victoria's personal doctor when she was in Scotland and became president of the Royal College of Surgeons of Edinburgh, but was never appointed professor at the Royal Infirmary.

After his marriage Bell and his wife lived at **5 Castle Terrace** *Map p124* **M13** (EH1 2DP), then moved to **20 Melville Street** *Map p120* **K13** (EH3 7NS) and lastly to **2 Melville Crescent** *Map p120* **K13** (now the Japanese consulate, plaque, EH3 7HW). He is buried in the **Dean Cemetery** *Map p120* **I11** (63 Dean Path, through Dean Path gates, turn right, left at last path, white marble cross, middle of north wall, bordering Ravelston Terrace, EH4 3AT). Displays are at the **Surgeons' Hall Museum** *Map p126* **R14** (18 Nicolson Street, artefacts, EH8 9DW).

With the success of the Sherlock Holmes stories, Bell got unwanted publicity. While he was proud of his former student, he also railed against '...the cataract of drivel for which Conan Doyle is responsible'.

Joseph Bell's academic robes at the Surgeons' Hall Museum *Map p126* **R14**.

∼ JOSEPH BLACK ∼

1728–99, SCIENTIST

Joseph Black was born in Bordeaux, one of thirteen children, where his Irish father was in the wine trade. His mother was Scottish, and he went first to the University of Glasgow at the age of eighteen, and then to the University of Edinburgh four years later to complete his studies in medicine. He became professor there in 1766, where he was a popular lecturer.

In about 1770 he amazed a group of friends, including James Hutton, q.v., by showing them a calf's foetal membrane, filled like a balloon, which rose to the ceiling. His friends searched for secret threads, but he had proven hydrogen is lighter than air; he had postulated that such balloons could allow flight. In 1785 the first manned hydrogen balloon in Scotland rose from the grounds of **Heriot's Hospital** Map p124 **P15** (now George Heriot's School, Lauriston Place, EH3 9EQ), watched by 80,000 spectators, when a young Italian, Vincenzo Lunardi, ascended three miles and returned safely.

An early invention in about 1780 was the analytical balance, far more precise than previous ones and therefore important for chemistry. Black then discovered 'fixed air', carbon dioxide, revolutionizing the understanding of respiration. In physics, he established the concepts of latent and specific heat, fundamental to thermodynamics and useful to his friend, James Watt, in his development of the steam engine.

Black first lived in **College Wynd** Map p124 **Q14** (now Guthrie Street, since demolished, near east corner with Chambers Street, EH1 1HR), then moved in 1744 to **Argyll Square** Map p124 **Q14** (since demolished, near National Museum of Scotland, Chambers Street, EH1 1JF) and finally to **58 Nicolson Street** Map p126 **R15** (since demolished, now supermarket, EH8 9DT). An archaeological dig at the **University of Edinburgh** Map p126 **R14** (Old College, South Bridge, EH8 9YL) unearthed apparatus and chemicals thought to have belonged to him. He never married but counted many Scottish Enlightenment figures among his friends, including David Hume, q.v., and

Adam Smith, q.v., who said, 'No man had less nonsense in his head than Dr Black.' He is considered a founding father of chemistry. His portrait and a medallion are in the **Scottish National Portrait Gallery** Map p122 **P10** (1 Queen Street, gallery 7, second floor, EH2 1JD), and a chemical balance is in the **National Museum of Scotland** Map p124 **Q14** (Chambers Street, 'Scotland Transformed', level 3, middle, EH1 1JF). He is buried in **Greyfriars Kirkyard** Map p124 **P14** (1 Greyfriars Place, South Yard, (section locked), EH1 2QQ).

The chemical balance invented by Joseph Black in about 1780, National Museum of Scotland Map p124 **Q14**.

WILLIAM DICK

1793–1866, VETERINARIAN

William Dick was born in **White Horse Close** *Map p118* **U12** (27 Canongate, Royal Mile, through archway, plaque between nos. 2 and 3, EH8 8BU), one of eight children of a blacksmith, and was baptized at **Trinity College Church** *Map p122* **Q12** (since demolished, site of Waverley Station, Waverley Bridge, EH1 1BB). Before the days of trained veterinarians, blacksmiths sometimes treated sick horses. As Dick helped his father, he learned about horses and became concerned for their welfare. The family moved to **Nottingham Place** *Map p118* **R10** (since demolished, near Greenside Row, EH1 3AJ) and then in 1815 to **15 Clyde Street** *Map p122* **P10** (since demolished, site of St Andrew Square Bus Station, plaque at bottom of escalator near St Andrew Square entrance, EH2 2AD). He started to attend the university's extramural lectures in mathematics and rhetoric, then in medicine. He wanted to learn more about animals, so also went to anatomy lectures, but found these insufficient. He went to veterinary college in London for three months and obtained a diploma.

Dick returned to Edinburgh and started giving lectures at the **Freemasons' Hall** *Map p126* **R13** (Niddry Street, corner of Cowgate, now St Cecilia's Hall, EH1 1LJ). Both students and farmers attended, with the syllabus covering the diseases and anatomy of farm animals. With the success of this enterprise, Dick was given £50 by the Highland Society to set up a 'systematic course in veterinary science'. Lectures were held at the **Calton Convening Rooms** *Map p118* **R11** (29 Waterloo Place, now a restaurant, EH1 3BQ) with the practical part of the course held at his father's premises as the Clyde Street Veterinary College, the first vet school in Scotland. Later he added his own money to enlarge it, and the former stable became an animal hospital. In 1844 they were granted a Royal Charter and became the Royal College of Veterinary Surgeons. Dick and his elder sister, Mary, still lived on an upper floor. He had been appointed Veterinary Surgeon in Scotland to Queen Victoria. By the time of his death, the over 800 students he had taught had set up at least six other veterinary colleges.

Besides running the college and lecturing, Dick maintained his own practice. He is commemorated at the University of Edinburgh's **Royal (Dick) School of Veterinary Studies** (off map, now at Easter Bush, EH25 9RG), with stained-glass windows, a sculpture of a horse and a statue. He is buried at **New Calton Burial Ground** *Map p118* **U11** (Regent Road, near centre, north-east of crossroads, red granite, EH8 8DR).

White Horse Close, the birthplace of William Dick
Map p118 **U12**.

~ SIR PATRICK GEDDES ~

1854–1932, FATHER OF TOWN PLANNING

Patrick Geddes was born in Ballater and brought up in Perth, before going to London to study biology with T. H. Huxley. He was appointed a lecturer in botany at the University of Edinburgh in 1880 although he had no degree, and lived at **81a Princes Street** *Map p122* **O12** (since demolished, 80–81 Princes Street, EH2 2ER). After he married Anna Morton, they moved to **6 James' Court** *Map p124* **P13** (493 Lawnmarket, Royal Mile, second-floor flat, EH1 2PB), then a slum, to show solidarity with ordinary people and to show by example that these buildings could be renovated. His interests included biology, sociology and philosophy, but he is best known as a town planner and educator.

He bought **Ramsay Lodge** *Map p124* **O13** (Ramsay Gardens, EH1 2NA), which had been the home of Allan Ramsay q.v., extended it and built other flats, which together became Ramsay Gardens. He then bought the nearby **Short's Observatory** *Map p124* **O13** (now the Camera Obscura, 549 Castlehill, Royal Mile, EH1 2ND) in 1892 with the object of exhibiting ideas for improving the environment, before moving to **14 Ramsay Gardens** *Map p124* **O13** (plaque, EH1 2NA) in 1893.

Geddes travelled widely and advised on town planning in India, started rural industries in Cyprus, did a lecture tour of the United States and founded the Scots College in Montpellier, France, where he lived from 1924 until his death. From 1927 he collaborated on the planning of **Edinburgh Zoo** (off map, 134 Corstorphine Road, EH12 6TS).

While he never actually said, 'Think global, act local', Geddes was an ecologist before his time. He believed in the unity of different branches of learning and in cooperative action. Instrumental in developing the first dedicated student residence in Scotland, **Mylne's Court** *Map p124* **P13** (now Patrick Geddes Hall, University of Edinburgh, 517 Lawnmarket, Royal Mile, plaque at entrance, EH1 2PF), he also ran summer schools and supported moral and spiritual development, especially with reference to the Celtic revival in art. As a town planner, he favoured diagnosis and renovation, rather than the usual slum clearance then prevalent, and was responsible for saving much of the Royal Mile. He is commemorated at **Waverley Court** *Map p118* **R12** (City of Edinburgh Council headquarters building, 4 East Market Street, stained glass, EH8 8BG) and the **Scottish National Portrait Gallery** *Map p122* **P10** (1 Queen Street, library, first floor, bust, EH2 1JD).

Stained-glass panel, Kate Henderson, left of entrance, City of Edinburgh Council headquarters building, Waverley Court *Map p118* **R12**.

~ PETER HIGGS ~

1929–, PHYSICIST

Peter Ware Higgs was born near Newcastle. As a child, his family moved frequently because of his father's job as a BBC sound engineer. After study at King's College, London, where he was awarded a PhD in physics, he took up a studentship at the University of Edinburgh in 1954, before returning to London two years later. But having fallen in love with Edinburgh while passing through in 1948, he returned in 1960 to become a lecturer at the Tait Institute of Mathematical Physics. Here he became interested in the physics of mass, in particular the search for the reason particles have mass. After spending his research career in this quest, he retired in 1996 and became Emeritus Professor of the University of Edinburgh.

Along with colleagues, he proposed in 1964 that an elementary particle gave mass to other ones. His hypothesis was that at the start of the universe, particles were without mass. His theoretical particle has become known as the Higgs boson or the God particle and has been the subject of experiments at the Large Hadron Collider at CERN near Geneva. Creating conditions similar to those just after the Big Bang, in 2012 they were able to show the likelihood of the existence of the elusive boson.

Higgs has received numerous awards for his work in theoretical physics, one of which was the Edinburgh Award in 2011, which meant that a flagstone with his hand prints was installed at the **City Chambers** *Map p124* **Q13** (Royal Mile, High Street, west side of entrance, EH1 1YJ).

His portrait hangs in the entrance of the University of Edinburgh's **James Clerk Maxwell Building** (off map, King's Buildings, Mayfield Road, turn off road, turn left, right and right, EH9 3JZ), and another is at the **Scottish National Portrait Gallery** *Map p122* **P10** (1 Queen Street, gallery 11, first floor, EH2 1JD). If the existence of the Higgs boson is proven, it is thought Higgs will be in line for a Nobel Prize in Physics. He lives in the New Town area of Edinburgh and has been included in the *44 Scotland Street* novels by Alexander McCall Smith, q.v.

The hand prints of Peter Higgs, City Chambers
Map p124 **Q13**.

PIONEERS

~ DAVID HUME ~

1711–76, PHILOSOPHER

David Hume was born at **Buchanan's Court** Map p124 **P13** (east of Brodie's Close, since demolished, near 300 Lawnmarket, Royal Mile, EH1 2PS), the younger son of a Berwickshire advocate. He studied law at the University of Edinburgh but found it 'nauseous' and left without a degree. He went to London in 1734 to study philosophy and later to France, where he published *A Treatise of Human Nature* at the age of twenty-six. Returning to Edinburgh, he was appointed Keeper of the **Advocates' Library** Map p124 **P13** (Parliament Square, EH1 1RF) in 1752, but quarrelled with the curators over books he wanted to order and resigned. During this time he bought his first house at **Riddle's Court** Map p124 **P13** (now 322 Lawnmarket, Royal Mile, EH1 2PG), where he lived with his sister, a maid and a cat, and published his *Political Discourses*. In 1753 he moved to **Jack's Land** Map p118 **S12** (now 229 Canongate, Royal Mile, opposite St John's Street, EH8 8BJ).

He again left Edinburgh for France, where he became a friend of Rousseau, returning in 1769. After briefly living at **James' Court** Map p124 **P13** (493 Lawnmarket, Royal Mile, destroyed by fire 1857, plaque at mid-entry, third storey of the western block, EH1 2PB), he had a house built in what became **South St David Street** Map p122 **P11** (now 21 South St David Street, carved in stone at first-floor level, north-east corner with St Andrew Square, EH2 2BW) named as a joke against the sceptic, where he lived until his death.

Since he argued for a reliance on the senses to gain knowledge of the world, he came into conflict with the Church. He also tried to divorce morality from its teachings and wrote that belief was a feeling, not a rational process. An empiricist, he contended that humans were driven by desire, not reason. He was charged with heresy, and his appointment as professor at the University of Edinburgh was blocked.

Hume enjoyed cooking for his friends, who included James Boswell, q.v., and Adam Smith, q.v., and the company of clever women. His huge work, *The History of England*, which took fifteen years to complete, made him wealthy. He died cheerfully, saying he did not fear oblivion. He is commemorated with a monument in the **Old Calton Burial Ground** Map p118 **R11** (27 Waterloo Place, David Hume Monument, south-west section, EH1 3BQ), in the **Scottish National Portrait Gallery** Map p122 **P10** (1 Queen Street, library, first floor, medallion; gallery 5, second floor, two portraits, EH2 1JD), and with a **statue** in front of the High Court of Justiciary Map p124 **P13** (by Alexander Stoddart, Lawnmarket, Royal Mile, north-east corner with Bank Street, EH1 2NT).

Statue of David Hume, outside the High Court of Justiciary, Royal Mile Map p124 **P13**.

～ JAMES HUTTON ～

1726–97, GEOLOGIST

James Hutton was born in Edinburgh. After attending the University of Edinburgh, he was apprenticed to a lawyer, but was dismissed for spending all his times on chemical experiments in the office. He then trained in medicine in Paris and Leiden but never practised. In 1759 he returned to Edinburgh and set up a business with a friend making smelling salts from coal soot, using a process they had invented. It was such a successful enterprise that by middle age he had the independence to pursue his real interest, geology.

The belief at the time was that the biblical Flood was the main geological force and that the Earth was about 6,000 years old. Hutton postulated that the Earth's core is molten. He said that the rock now called igneous could have been formed only by heat. He further founded the theory of uniformitarianism, which hypothesizes that geological processes occur over vast periods of time and that these same processes are unvarying and can be observed to the present day.

In 1770 Hutton built himself a house at **St John's Hill** Map p126 **S13** (EH8 9TS), where he lived with his three sisters until his death. He wrote the *Theory of the Earth* over twenty-five years and presented a summary of it to the **Royal Society of Edinburgh** Map p126 **R14** (initially met at University of Edinburgh, Old College, South Bridge, EH8 9YL) in 1785.

A part of Salisbury Crags at Holyrood Park, where he observed volcanic rock, is known as **Hutton's Section** Map p126 **V16** (Salisbury Crags, near Pollock Halls of Residence, University of Edinburgh, 18 Holyrood Park Road, interpretation board, EH16 5AY). He is commemorated at the **Hutton Memorial Garden** Map p126 **S13** (accessed by steps up from Viewcraig Gardens, off Holyrood Road, EH8 9UQ), and with a plaque at the **University of Edinburgh's Grant Institute of Earth Sciences** (off map, plaque at entrance of building, King's Buildings, West Mains Road, EH9 3JW). His portrait is in the **Scottish National Portrait Gallery** Map p122 **P10** (1 Queen Street, gallery 7, second floor, EH2 1JD). He is buried in **Greyfriars Kirkyard** Map p124 **P14** (1 Greyfriars Place, white marble plaque, South Yard, east side (section locked), EH1 2QQ).

His other interests ranged from canal building to meteorology, both of which he

investigated, but his most significant contribution was his theories of geology, slightly modified versions of which are still accepted today. His enduring hypotheses mean that he is known as the founding father of modern geology.

The Hutton Memorial Garden
Map p126 **S13**.

PIONEERS

Dr Elsie Inglis

1864–1917, SURGEON AND SUFFRAGIST

Eliza Maud Inglis was born in India. She and her family came to Edinburgh in 1878, where they lived at **10 Bruntsfield Place** *Map p128* **M17** (EH10 4HN), and she attended the **Edinburgh Institution for the Education of Young Ladies** *Map p120* **L12** (23 Charlotte Square, EH2 4DF). Her enlightened parents allowed her to consider medical training, and she began her studies at the newly created **Edinburgh School of Medicine for Women** *Map p126* **R14** (Surgeons' Square, High School Yards, now part of University of Edinburgh, bear right and through archway, EH1 1LZ) and later graduated from the University of Edinburgh as one of its first female medical students. In 1902 she opened a hospital for poor mothers and children, staffed by women, at **11 George Square** *Map p124* **Q16** (since demolished, now the Hugh Robson Building, EH8 9XD). It moved to the **Royal Mile** *Map p124* **Q13** (219 High Street, Royal Mile, two plaques at first floor level, EH1 1PE), where it became known as the Hospice, and then became the **Elsie Inglis Memorial Maternity Hospital** *Map p118* **W11** (since partly demolished, Spring Gardens, Abbeyhill, EH8 8EW) after her death. Concern for the welfare of the poorest meant she would waive her fee when necessary. At the same time, she practised medicine at **8 Walker Street** *Map p120* **K13** (carved in stone, EH3 7LH) and lectured at the **Medical College for Women** *Map p124* **Q14** (30 Chambers Street, now pub and offices, EH1 1HU), which she had helped to found in 1894.

Increasingly interested in the women's suffrage movement, Inglis addressed numerous meetings and became secretary of the non-militant Federation of Scottish Suffrage Societies. Much of her dissatisfaction was about poor standards of medical care for women. When war broke out in 1914, she wanted to send women doctors to the front. The British government rejected her offer, but she was welcomed by the French and Serbians. She set up several all-women hospital units in Serbia to attend to Allied casualties. Serbia honoured her with its highest award, given to a woman for the first time. She died of cancer the day after returning to Britain. Her body lay in state at St Giles Cathedral, before burial at the **Dean Cemetery** *Map p120* **I11** (63 Dean Path, through Dean Path gates, turn right, left at third path, right at fifth path, first on right, Celtic cross, EH4 3AT).

Inglis is commemorated at **St Giles Cathedral** *Map p124* **Q13** (Royal Mile, north-east area, carved plaque, EH1 1RE), with a bust in the **Scottish National Portrait Gallery** *Map p122* **P10** (1 Queen Street, gallery 11, first floor, EH2 1JD), at the **National War Museum** *Map p124* **N13** (Edinburgh Castle, Castlehill, 'Women at War', ground floor, collecting box, EH1 2NG), and with a plaque at the **Old Surgeons' Hall** *Map p126* **R14** (Surgeons' Square, High School Yards, now part of University of Edinburgh, bear right and through archway, EH1 1LZ).

Collecting box for the organization formed by Elsie Inglis, National War Museum, Edinburgh Castle *Map p124* **N13**.

PIONEERS

~ Dr Sophia Jex-Blake ~

1840–1912, DOCTOR AND HOSPITAL FOUNDER

Sophia Jex-Blake was born into a medical family in Hastings. After qualifying as a teacher, she came to Edinburgh in 1872 and, with a small number of other women, attended extra-mural lectures in medicine at the Royal Colleges of Physicians and Surgeons. She had to go to Switzerland to qualify and then obtained her licence to practise from Ireland, becoming the third woman to be registered as a doctor in Britain.

After helping to found a women's medical college in London, she returned to Edinburgh in 1878 and set up a practice at her home at **4 Manor Place** Map p120 **K14** (EH3 7DD), soon expanding to become the Edinburgh Hospital and Dispensary for Women and Children at **6 Grove Street** Map p120 **K15** (EH3 8BB), in a deprived area, later moving to **73 Grove Street** Map p120 **K16** (EH3 8FG). With women still barred from medical training, she opened her own small medical school in 1886, the Edinburgh School of Medicine for Women, which moved the following year to **Surgeons' Square** Map p126 **R14** (High School Yards, now part of University of Edinburgh, bear right and through archway, EH1 1LZ). She was the first female medical lecturer in Scotland. When her female students were refused permission to do their clinical training at the Royal Infirmary, Jex-Blake found **Leith Hospital** Map p118 **T2** (8–10 Mill Lane, now closed, EH6 6TJ) more accommodating. By this time she was living at Bruntsfield Lodge, which now became first a dispensary and then the **Edinburgh Hospital for Women and Children** Map p128 **N19** (now flats, plaque, 90–94 Whitehouse Loan, south-west corner with Bruntsfield Crescent, EH9 1BD), catering for poor women and their children, which closed only in 1989.

Unsurprisingly, Jex-Blake was an unconventional and strong-minded woman. She had to campaign against fierce opposition for women to be admitted to medical school, only fully implemented at the University of Edinburgh in 1894. A strict disciplinarian, she also did not attend church regularly and drove her own pony and trap. With one of her students, Elsie Inglis, q.v., she supported women's suffrage.

After retirement, Jex-Blake returned to Sussex, where she died. She is commemorated in **St Giles Cathedral** Map p124 **Q13** (Royal Mile, north-east area, Chambers aisle, EH1 1RE), and with a plaque at the **University of Edinburgh** Map p124 **Q15** (Old Medical School, Teviot Place, plaque within archway on left, EH8 9AG).

The plaque honouring Sophia Jex-Blake at the Old Medical School, University of Edinburgh Map p124 **Q15**.

～ JOHN KNOX ～

C.1505–15–1572, THEOLOGIAN

John Knox was born near Haddington and probably studied at Glasgow or St Andrews, before being ordained as a priest and becoming a papal notary (lawyer). Almost immediately he started to view Catholicism as idolatry and embraced the new concept of Protestantism. In 1547 he was preaching in St Andrews when religious opponents fought and killed each other. Knox was captured and was a galley slave for nineteen months, before he escaped or was released.

He went to live in England, Frankfurt and Geneva, where he met John Calvin, and formulated many of the doctrines that would become the basis of Scottish Presbyterianism, including predestination, the elect and original sin. He visited Edinburgh twice, preached in private and tried to influence the aristocracy with his religious ideas. Because Scotland was a separate country, Henry VIII's reforms had had no impact, but by 1560 the Scottish Parliament had decided on religious reform and so banned Catholic practice. Knox was appointed minister of **St Giles Kirk** *Map p124* **Q13** (now St Giles Cathedral, Royal Mile, EH1 1RE) and remained there until his death. He lived at **Warriston's Close** *Map p124* **Q13** (west of City Chambers, 323 High Street, Royal Mile, EH1 1PG) between 1560 and 1566, then returned to England for six years. He came back to Edinburgh and preached one last time before his death at **John Knox House** *Map p126* **R13** (43–45 High Street, Royal Mile, EH1 1SR).

His many writings include *First Blast of the Trumpet against the Monstrous Regiment of Women*, opposing women rulers, in particular Mary Queen of Scots, q.v., with whom he clashed. Considering himself like an Old Testament prophet, he stripped churches of decoration and ceremony. He has been called joyless and narrow-minded, but he also supported universal education and a programme of poor relief. He married a seventeen-year-old when he was about fifty and enjoyed music, the theatre and dancing.

Knox is buried under what is now the car park beside **St Giles Cathedral** *Map p124* **Q13** (Royal Mile, south of cathedral, brass square at no. 23 parking space; statue in north aisle of cathedral near entrance, EH1 1RE), and is commemorated with another statue at the **Assembly Hall** *Map p124* **P13** (Mound Place, EH1 2LU), and with an engraving in the **Scottish National Portrait Gallery** *Map p122* **P10** (1 Queen Street, gallery 1, second floor, EH2 1JD).

A detail on John Knox House, where Knox died *Map p126* **R13**.

PIONEERS

PROF JOSEPH LISTER (LORD LISTER)

1827–1912, SURGEON

Joseph Lister was born into a Quaker family near London. After graduating in medicine at the University of London, he went to Edinburgh for surgical studies with James Syme, who became his father-in-law. The marriage to Agnes took place at the family home at **Millbank** Map p128 **N22** (since demolished, Millbank Pavilion on same site in the grounds of Astley Ainslie Hospital, 133 Grange Loan, EH9 2HL) in 1856. Their first marital home was at **11 Rutland Square** Map p120 **L13** (carved in stone, EH1 2AS).

Lister practised surgery at the **Royal Infirmary** Map p124 **P15** (now Quartermile, 1 Lauriston Place, EH3 9AU) and lectured at the **Royal College of Surgeons** Map p126 **R14** (Surgeons' Square, High School Yards, now part of University of Edinburgh, bear right and through archway, EH1 1LZ). At the same time he was reading about Louis Pasteur's research into infection and how carbolic acid could neutralize sewage. He combined these ideas and introduced carbolic spray as a disinfectant in operations, to clean wounds and sterilize surgical instruments. The death rate reduced dramatically. Routine cleanliness such as hand washing was not then a standard part of hospital practice, but Lister instituted a new regime.

After a spell as the Regius Professor of Surgery at Glasgow, he became Professor of Clinical Surgery at the University of Edinburgh in 1869. He developed effective dressings for wounds, using muslin gauze found at a draper's shop, and continued to develop techniques to improve antisepsis. He was created a baronet in 1883 and raised to the peerage as a baron in 1897.

In later years his fame was such that members of the public would come to hear him lecture, and he became known as the father of antisepsis. Both the bacterium listeria and Listerine mouthwash are named in honour of him, although he had no direct connection with either. When King Edward VII was diagnosed with appendicitis two days before his coronation, Lister advised on what was still a risky intervention. The king credited Lister with his survival.

In later years he lived at **9 Charlotte Square** Map p120 **L12** (carved in stone, EH2 4DR), before returning to London in 1877, where he died. Artefacts are at the **Surgeons' Hall Museum** Map p126 **R14** (18 Nicolson Street, EH8 9DW) and a plaque at the **University of Edinburgh** Map p124 **Q15** (Old Medical School, Teviot Place, plaque within archway on left, EH8 9AG).

One of Joseph Lister's instruments to spray antiseptic, Surgeons' Hall Museum Map p126 **R14**.

PIONEERS

SIR HENRY LITTLEJOHN

1826–1914, DOCTOR

Henry Duncan Littlejohn and his twin sister Helen were born in Edinburgh. Their father died young, and he lived with his widowed mother and five siblings at **2 Elder Street** Map p122 **Q10** (EH1 3DX). Littlejohn trained at the **Edinburgh Medical School** Map p126 **R14** (University of Edinburgh, Old College, South Bridge, EH8 9YL) before becoming Edinburgh's first Medical Officer of Health in 1862, serving in the post until his retirement in 1908.

A tenement at **Paisley Close** Map p126 **R13** (101 High Street, Royal Mile, north side, carving over close entrance, EH1 1SP) had collapsed the previous year, killing thirty-five people, but a boy who was trapped had called out to rescuers, 'Heave awa', lads, I'm no deid yet.' The now-Anglicized phase is memorialized with a carved inscription there, but people were shocked at the overcrowding and appalling living conditions and wanted a solution.

Littlejohn took the view that infectious diseases were the result of poverty, lack of sanitation and poor housing. In 1865 he published his *Report on the Sanitary Conditions of the City of Edinburgh*. His reforms, for example requiring abattoirs and cattle markets to be moved out of town, and other measures such as the legal requirement to notify cases of certain infectious diseases, were instrumental in dramatically reducing the incidence of cholera, typhus and smallpox. This system of making diseases notifiable was adopted nationally.

At the same time, he was a police surgeon and medical advisor to the Crown for criminal cases in Scotland, for example in the 1889 trial of Jessie King, q.v. Often called as an expert witness, he developed scientific forensic techniques for the analysis of evidence. Arthur Conan Doyle, q.v., cited Joseph Bell, q.v., as his primary source for Sherlock Holmes, but Littlejohn's methods were credited with contributing to the inspiration for this enduring character. During this time he and his family lived first at **40 York Place** Map p122 **Q10** (since demolished, now St Paul's and St George's Church, EH1 3HU), and then from 1866 until his death at **24 Royal Circus** Map p122 **M9** (plaque, EH3 6SS). Littlejohn is buried at the **Dean Cemetery** Map p120 **I11** (63 Dean Path, through Dean Path gates, turn left, first path on right, bear left, near back of cemetery on left, EH4 3AT), and commemorated at the **Surgeons' Hall Museum** Map p126 **R14** (18 Nicolson Street, EH8 9DW).

The carved inscription and head of a boy at Paisley Close, Royal Mile, where a tenement had collapsed Map p126 **R13**.

PIONEERS

— James Clerk Maxwell —

1831–79, MATHEMATICIAN AND PHYSICIST

James Clerk was born at **14 India Street** *Map p122* **M10** (carved in stone between ground-floor windows, EH3 6EZ), the only surviving child of wealthy parents. He acquired his surname when he inherited a country estate because of his connections with the Maxwell family. The family spent much of his childhood there in Dumfries and Galloway. When he went to **Edinburgh Academy** *Map p116* **M8** (42 Henderson Row, includes James Clerk Maxwell Science Centre, EH3 5BL), boarding during term time with his aunt at **31 Heriot Row** *Map p122* **N10** (EH3 6ES), he was called Dafty because of his small stature and broad accent. He went on to the **University of Edinburgh** *Map p126* **R14** (Old College, South Bridge, EH8 9YL) in 1847, before going to Cambridge, where he later became the first professor of experimental physics.

From childhood, Maxwell was intensely curious about the natural world, collecting flowers and insects and studying them seriously. He published his first paper, *On the Description of Oval Curves*, at fifteen. His particular interests became electricity, magnetism and optics, which he showed were all related. His *magnum opus*, *A Treatise on Electricity and Magnetism*, published in 1873, named electromagnetism as the overall phenomenon and predicted the existence of waves travelling at the speed of light. Fascinated by the rings of Saturn, he postulated that they were neither entirely solid nor liquid, but made of small particles. His theory was proven correct in the 1980s when the *Voyager* spaceship made close observations. He also worked on the measurement of colour, analyzing colour perception and producing the first durable colour photograph in 1861.

Maxwell's equations were the foundation stones for modern physics and allowed the later development of radio, television and radar. He is considered the father of electronics. Even current work trying to create cloaks of invisibility relies on them, and Einstein ranked him as the most important scientist of the nineteenth century. His statue is in **George Street** *Map p122* **P11** (George Street at St Andrew Square, EH2 2LL), his photo in the **Scottish National Portrait Gallery** *Map p122* **P10** (1 Queen Street, gallery 11, first floor, photo, model of statue, EH2 1JD), and one of his instruments in the **National Museum of Scotland** *Map p124* **Q14** (Chambers Street, 'Shaping Our World', level 5, instrument with dynamic top and colour sectors, EH1 1JF). He died in Cambridge and is buried near the family estate.

The statue of James Clerk Maxwell, holding a spinning colour top, George Street at St Andrew Square *Map p122* **P11**.

～ HUGH MILLER ～

1802–56, STONEMASON AND WRITER

Hugh Miller was born in Cromarty, coming to Edinburgh in 1820 to try to sell some family property in Leith. He had been apprenticed as a stonemason and took up work on an extension to **Niddrie House** (off map, since demolished, now Jack Kane Sports Centre, 208 Niddrie Mains Road, EH16 4NB). He read extensively, especially about geology, and would look for specimens in **Holyrood Park** Map p126 **V13** (EH16 5BT). However, his work caused him to suffer from pneumoconiosis, a lung disease, and he turned to writing about poetry and theology, and later geology. He was also active in the foundation of the Free Church of Scotland. His prominence in both fields meant that in 1840 he was invited to edit *The Witness*, an evangelical publication, but which included a wide variety of subject matter, whose offices were in the **Royal Mile** Map p124 **Q13** (297 High Street, Royal Mile, since demolished, plaque at City Chambers, EH1 1YJ). He lived at **Archibald Place** Map p124 **O15** (since demolished, now side of Edinburgh Postgraduate Dental Institute, Lauriston Place, EH3 9HA) and later at **Stuart Street** (off map, now Abercorn Gardens, EH8 7BJ).

At the same time, Miller published *The Old Red Sandstone*, a collection of his popular science essays from *The Witness*, his autobiography and over forty other works over his lifetime, becoming an important literary figure. In his writings about geology, he emphasized the hand of a benevolent Creator, although he differed from current beliefs as well. He stated that the Earth was of a great age, that species had arisen and become extinct and that the Flood had been limited to the Middle East.

In 1852 he and his family moved to **Shrub Mount** (off map, behind 80 Portobello High Street, EH15 1AN) in Portobello, where he created a museum of geology and gave lectures on the subject locally. However, he started to suffer from severe headaches and paranoia, which

resulted in his carrying a revolver and erecting a mantrap in his garden. Fearing he was going mad, he shot himself, leaving a note saying, 'My brain burns.'

Shops closed while his huge funeral cortège made its way to the **Grange Cemetery** Map p128 **P20** (60a Grange Road, monument to left near Beaufort Road entrance, EH9 1TT). He is remembered with a bust at the **Scottish National Portrait Gallery** Map p122 **P10** (1 Queen Street, entrance hall, EH2 1JD), and a statue in the **National Museum of Scotland** Map p124 **Q14** (Chambers Street, 'Traditions in Sculpture', level 5, EH1 1JF).

Statue of Hugh Miller examining a fossil, National Museum of Scotland Map p124 **Q14**.

JOHN NAPIER OF MERCHISTON

1550–1617, MATHEMATICIAN

John Napier (also known as Neper) was born at **Merchiston Castle** _Map p128_ **K20** (also called Merchiston Tower, carved stone over door, now part of Edinburgh Napier University, Merchiston Campus, Colinton Road, EH10 5DT), which had been in the family since 1438, and became its eighth laird. He studied at St Andrews University, but left without a degree and possibly went abroad for further education.

As an early and fanatical Protestant, Napier wrote about religion, in particular against Roman Catholicism, and was also worried about an invasion by Catholic Spain. His inventions include an early version of a tank, a submarine and a mirror to burn enemy ships. He also turned his mind to more domestic matters, working on a hydraulic screw to clear flooded mines and new ways of farming, such as using salt as a fertilizer. Other interests included alchemy, astrology, astronomy, magic and mathematics, all thought to be connected at the time. Some thought he was a wizard, but he just used his scientific knowledge and intelligence to mystify the credulous.

Napier invented the concept of logarithms, a valuable tool for mathematicians to simplify calculation. He spent twenty years constructing the tables, which became the basis of scientific and engineering calculation until the advent of the computer. A further important contribution was the decimal point and the system of writing decimal fractions still in use today. He further devised two calculating 'machines', one of which is known as Napier's bones. With numbers carved into them, these ivory rods are a type of abacus or slide rule and could be used to quickly and accurately do arithmetic calculations, including square and cube roots.

Napier was twice married, had ten children and died at his home. A loner, he could sometimes be seen wearing a long, black cloak while walking with his dog. He is buried at **St Cuthbert's Church** _Map p124_ **M13** (memorial stone in church vestibule, right-hand side, 5 Lothian Road, EH1 2EP), his calculating machines are in the **National Museum of Scotland** _Map p124_ **Q14** (Chambers Street, 'Kingdom of the Scots', level 1, north-west section, also touchscreen, EH1 1JF) and a sculpture at **Napier University** (off map, Craighouse Campus, Craighouse Road, in front of New Craig building, EH10 5LG). His contributions allowed many scientific advances, and he is considered a precursor of computer science.

Napier's bones, c.1650, National Museum of Scotland _Map p124_ **Q14**.

⁓ Dr James Young Simpson ⁓

1811–70, OBSTETRICIAN

James Young Simpson was the youngest of seven sons of a baker in Bathgate near Edinburgh. When he went to the University of Edinburgh at the age of fourteen to study medicine, he was appalled by the horrors of operating without anaesthesia and considered giving up. When he later became a house surgeon at the Lying-in (Maternity) Hospital in Leith, he was again struck by the pain suffered by the poor, sick or abandoned women he attended.

He was appointed Professor of Midwifery in 1839, aged only twenty-eight and the youngest ever, despite professional hostility because of his humble origins, a post he retained until his death. He made many scientific discoveries while remaining a working doctor, ready to treat all classes of people, with a medical dispensary in **Carrubber's Close** Map p126 **R13** (High Street, off the Royal Mile, EH1 1SJ).

His most important breakthrough was in anaesthetics and happened at the dining table of his home at **52 Queen Street** Map p122 **N11** (carved in stone, EH2 3NS) in 1847. With several friends he inhaled various fluids, one of which he had obtained from a chemist at **52 North Bridge** Map p122 **Q12** (since demolished, now the side of the Balmoral Hotel, North Bridge, near Princes Street, plaque, EH2 2EQ). When he and his colleagues all crashed to the floor, he realized that chloroform was the substance he had been looking for.

He administered chloroform to a woman in labour four days later. It was almost immediately accepted as useful for surgery, but was opposed by the profession for childbirth until it was administered to Queen Victoria as she gave birth to Prince Leopold in 1853. He was created the Physician to the Queen in Scotland, then made a baronet in 1866. Simpson is considered to be the father of anaesthetics and to have founded the modern practice of gynaecology, with new methods, diagnoses and advances in obstetrics.

He is commemorated with a statue in **West Princes Street Gardens** Map p124 **M13** (Princes Street, near back of Church of St John the Evangelist, EH2 4BJ) at the **Surgeons' Hall Museum** Map p126 **R14** (18 Nicolson Street, decanter, EH8 9DW), the **University of Edinburgh** Map p124 **Q15** (Old Medical School, plaque left side within entrance archway, Teviot Place, EH8 9AG), and in **St Giles Cathedral** Map p124 **Q13** (Royal Mile, south aisle, EH1 1RE). He is buried at **Warriston Cemetery** Map p116 **O4** (42 Warriston Gardens, through gates, fourth turning on left, end of wooden fence, right side, obelisk on steep slope, EH3 5NE).

James Young Simpson's chloroform decanter, Surgeons' Hall Museum Map p126 **R14**.

∼ ADAM SMITH ∼

1723–90, ECONOMIST

Adam Smith was born in Kirkcaldy, his father a lawyer who had died before he was born. A sickly child, he also had the trauma of being abducted at the age of three, before being rescued almost immediately by a relative. He was educated at Glasgow and Balliol College, Oxford, then returned to Kirkcaldy.

Between 1748 and 1751 he gave public lectures on rhetoric in Edinburgh, then went on to be a professor at Glasgow, but resigned his chair in 1763 to become the tutor to the young Duke of Buccleuch. In the meantime he had published his *Theory of Moral Sentiments* in 1759, in which he stated that morals should not be based on the precepts of theology. He believed there was no connection between morality and Christianity. Unsurprisingly it caused a sensation. His most famous work, *The Wealth of Nations*, followed in 1776. In it he was the first person to set out the idea of a free-market economy, proposing that economic self-interest was the basis of the public good and explaining how the division of labour could improve productivity. But he also opposed slavery and believed that freeing colonies would increase the prosperity of both colonizers and former colonies. He claimed that 'riches are a mere deception, but none the less they keep in motion the industry of mankind'. *The Wealth of Nations* has been called the most influential book on economics ever written, and Smith the first political economist. His output was published by William Creech at the **Luckenbooths** *Map p124* **Q13** (since demolished, middle of the Royal Mile near St Giles Cathedral, bookshop east end, EH1 1RE).

Smith lived at **Panmure House** *Map p118* **T12** (129 Canongate, Royal Mile, plaque, north side; access by walking east down the Royal Mile to next opening on left (Little Lochend Close, not signposted), building on left, EH8 8BL) from 1778 until his death. A shy, clumsy and absent-minded man, he never married. Shortly before his death he sent for his friends David Hume, q.v., and Joseph Black, q.v., asking them to burn sixteen volumes of his writings, which they did. He is buried at the **Canongate Kirk** *Map p118* **T12** (153 Canongate, Royal Mile, left side of entrance, south-west corner, EH8 8BN). A **statue** *Map p124* **Q13** (Royal Mile, near St Giles Cathedral, EH1 1RE) is in the Royal Mile, and portraits in the **Scottish National Portrait Gallery** *Map p122* **P10** (1 Queen Street, gallery 5, second floor, medallion; gallery 7, second floor, print, EH2 1JD).

Statue by Alexander Stoddart, Royal Mile, near St Giles Cathedral *Map p124* **Q13**.

PIONEERS

5

DOERS

If we were to follow the example of the doers in this section, we would never spend more than five minutes on the sofa. From soldiers to politicians, from athletes to entrepreneurs, they got on their bikes, sometimes literally, and did their best to change the world or at least a little bit of it.

Royalty features prominently. In the first millennium, Queen Margaret, who was to become St Margaret, wanted to change what she saw as outmoded practices in the Church. Mary Queen of Scots' desire for greater power led to her execution as a traitor. Her son, James VI and I, however, succeeded to the throne, so Mary's efforts were not all in vain. Bonnie Prince Charlie was less successful.

By the late nineteenth century, commoners were more likely to be in charge. Douglas Haig, later Earl Haig, became Commander-in-Chief of the troops during World War I, but was considered responsible for heavy casualties. In a different type of war, the socialist James Connolly was a leader of the 1916 Easter Rising in Ireland and was executed for his part in it. In more pacifist mode, Chrystal Macmillan was a peace campaigner and also took up the fight for women's rights.

Entrepreneurs started to make their mark at the same time. John Menzies opened a bookshop, then had the novel idea of putting bookstalls into railway stations. Not quite an entrepreneur, but someone who worked with them, Thomas Telford built bridges and other huge structures which still dominate the landscape. Roy Thomson, later Lord Thomson of Fleet, became one of the early press barons. Currently a crop of innovative chefs, including Michelin-starred Tom Kitchin, has helped to populate Edinburgh with excellent restaurants.

Doers of another stripe have fought other types of battle. Ludovic Kennedy took up hopeless causes of people wrongly convicted of crimes. Hamish Henderson championed and collected the music of outcasts such as traveller people and wrote stirring songs. Richard Demarco tirelessly brings innovative theatre and art to a wider audience.

Among the most active are athletes. Eric Liddell was an Olympic runner, who is best remembered for refusing to run on a Sunday because of his Christian faith. The cyclist Sir Chris Hoy has also achieved Olympic gold, while Yvonne Murray was another champion runner. Gavin Hastings has been called Scotland's best ever rugby player.

The goal of most politicians is to change the world for the better, although some would suggest that few succeed in their aim. As Labour Prime Minister, Tony Blair is most remembered for leading Britain into the Iraq war, but he also introduced the minimum wage. Sir Malcolm Rifkind, a Conservative, initially supported Margaret Thatcher's poll tax, but is also committed to the elimination of nuclear weapons.

We may not support all the causes or activities favoured by these doers, but at least their determination and stamina must be admired.

The Palace of Holyroodhouse, where royals have plotted or reigned benignly. *Map p118* **V12**.

DOERS

~ TONY BLAIR ~

1953–, POLITICIAN

Anthony Charles Lynton Blair was born at **5 Paisley Terrace** (off map, EH8 7JW) and spent the first nineteen months of his life there, before his father got a job at the University of Adelaide, where he lectured in law. They returned to Durham, and from 1966 until 1971 Blair boarded at **Fettes College** Map p116 **H7** (Carrington Road, EH4 1QX), having won a scholarship. A difficult student, he was obsessed with rock music and enjoyed going to the **Usher Hall** Map p124 **M14** (Lothian Road, EH1 2EA) to see pop groups. After graduation and a spell in London, he went to Oxford and earned a degree in law.

He soon joined the Labour Party and by 1983 had become the MP for the newly created seat of Sedgefield, near Durham. In 1994, by which time he had risen to become Shadow Home Secretary, the leader of the Labour Party, John Smith, died suddenly. Blair decided to stand for the leadership. He held secret meetings, including ones with his rival Gordon Brown, at **7 Randolph Cliff** Map p120 **K12** (EH3 7TZ), the home of the parents of his first love at Fettes, Amanda Mackenzie Stuart. He was elected Labour Party leader and went on to win the general election in 1997 with a landslide, remaining in post for ten years, making him Labour's longest-serving Prime Minister.

Blair is remembered for taking Britain into the controversial war in Iraq in 2003, part of the War on Terror as conceived by President George W. Bush, but opposed by many of his own MPs and much of the electorate. On the other hand, he did much to reform the Labour Party, introduced the minimum wage and more rights for gay people. He is credited with helping to end thirty years of conflict in Northern Ireland and being instrumental in ending the war in Kosovo. After his resignation, he became the United Nations Middle East envoy, trying to broker a settlement between Israel and the Palestinians. He lives in London with his family.

DOERS

The imposing Fettes College, Carrington Road Map p116 **H7**.

～ BONNIE PRINCE CHARLIE ～

1720–88, PRETENDER TO THE THRONE

When Queen Anne died in 1714 without a direct heir, Parliament invited the Protestant who became George I to succeed her, even through he was only fifty-second in line. Many believed that James Stuart should have been crowned, but as a Catholic this was impossible.

His son, Prince Charles Edward Louis John Casimir Sylvester Severino Maria Stuart, was born in Rome. In 1745 Bonnie Prince Charlie, as he became known, went to the Highlands to raise an army to support his father's goal of becoming king. His followers became known as Jacobites, for the Latin name of the last Stuart king. He was warmly welcomed, and later that year he reached Edinburgh. Some of his men hid outside the city gates at the **Netherbow Port** Map p126 **R13** (since demolished, near 4 High Street, Royal Mile, brass markers in road, corner of St Mary's Street, EH1 1TB), rushing in when the guards let a coach out. They ran up the Royal Mile to take the city. The rest of the Jacobite army made its way from the south-west to the **Palace of Holyroodhouse** Map p118 **V12** (Canongate, Royal Mile, EH8 8DX). The following day, Prince Charlie rode into town wearing Highland dress, cheered by 20,000 people. He proclaimed his father King James VIII and himself Prince Regent at the **Mercat Cross** Map p124 **Q13** (since demolished, near City Chambers, 253 High Street, Royal Mile, octagon shape in the paving, EH1 1YJ). He immediately left Edinburgh and stayed the night at a **Duddingston tavern** (off map, Prince Charlie's House, 8–10 The Causeway, at Duddingston Road West and Old Church Lane, carved in stone, EH15 3PZ). The following day they engaged Sir John Cope at the battle of Prestonpans and won convincingly. They had some further successes but were eventually defeated in 1746 at Culloden. Prince Charlie escaped to the Isle of Skye dressed as a woman, and was taken to France. He died in Rome, a disillusioned alcoholic.

Bonnie Prince Charlie and his men occupied Edinburgh for only six weeks. During that time some of his officers made their headquarters at the **White Horse Inn** Map p118 **U12** (now closed, White Horse Close, 27 Canongate, Royal Mile, EH8 8BU), and the Countess of Eglinton entertained Prince Charlie at her home at **Jack's Land** Map p118 **S12** (now 229 Canongate, Royal Mile, opposite St John's Street, EH8 8BJ). Artefacts can be seen in the **National Museum of Scotland** Map p124 **Q14** (Chambers Street, 'Scotland Transformed', level 3, east, silver travelling canteen, targe (shield), EH1 1JF), with five portraits and a bust at the **Scottish National Portrait Gallery** Map p122 **P10** (1 Queen Street, gallery 4, second floor, EH2 1JD).

Silver travelling canteen, possibly a twenty-first birthday present, National Museum of Scotland Map p124 **Q14**.

DOERS

～ James Connolly ～

1868–1916, TRADES UNIONIST AND POLITICIAN

James Connolly was born at **107 Cowgate** *Map p126* **R13** (plaque south-east abutment of George IV Bridge, beside 69 Cowgate, EH1 1JW), the son of impoverished Irish immigrants, his father a manure carter. The family moved to **2a King's Stables Road** *Map p124* **O14** (EH1 2JY), and he attended **St Patrick's Roman Catholic School** *Map p126* **R13** (since demolished, south of St Patrick's Church, near Cowgate, EH1 1TQ), leaving at eleven to take jobs as a printer's devil and baker's apprentice. At fourteen, he lied about his age and joined the army, serving in Ireland for seven years, before deserting when he was to be posted to India. He had observed the mistreatment of the Irish people by the British and landlords. In 1890, he and his new wife, Lily, were living at **22 West Port** *Map p124* **O14** (EH1 2JE). When he spoke at a rally in support of the eight-hour day, he was fired from his job with Edinburgh Corporation. In 1895 he briefly ran a cobbler's shop at **73 Buccleuch Street** *Map p126* **R16** (now lawyers' office, EH8 9LS).

Influenced by his brother he became involved with the Scottish Socialist Federation and the Independent Labour Party, the latter formed by Keir Hardie. In 1896 he went to Ireland and helped to found the Irish Socialist Party. He travelled extensively in Ireland, Scotland and the USA, proselytizing, and was a co-founder of the Labour Party in 1913.

Back in Ireland in 1916, he took part in the preparations for the Easter Rising, one of seven signatories to the proclamation that called for the end of British rule. In the fighting that followed, he was severely wounded. After the surrender, he was arrested and court martialed, when he was sentenced to death. He was thought to have only a few days to live and was too ill to stand, so was taken by ambulance to the Kilmainham Jail, tied to a chair and executed by firing squad.

The execution of a gravely wounded man was controversial and aroused the sympathies of Irish people who had not previously supported the uprising. Connolly is remembered as a socialist thinker and champion of the rights of ordinary people and Irish independence.

TO THE MEMORY OF JAMES CONNOLLY
BORN 6TH JUNE 1868 AT 107 COWGATE
RENOWNED INTERNATIONAL TRADE UNION
AND WORKING CLASS LEADER
FOUNDER OF IRISH SOCIALIST REPUBLICAN PARTY
MEMBER OF PROVISIONAL GOVERNMENT
OF IRISH REPUBLIC
EXECUTED 12TH MAY 1916 AT KILMAINHAM JAIL DUBLIN

The plaque near the birthplace of James Connolly in the Cowgate *Map p126* **R13**.

DOERS

RICHARD DEMARCO

1930–, ARTS PROMOTER AND ARTIST

Ricardo Demarco was born at **9 Grosvenor Street** *Map p120* **J14** (EH12 5ED), the son of Italian immigrants. The family soon moved to **9 Bath Street** (off map, EH15 1EZ) in Portobello. Demarco studied at **Edinburgh College of Art** *Map p124* **O15** (74 Lauriston Place, EH3 9DF) and became a painter and an art teacher at **Scotus Academy** (off map, 122 Corstorphine Road, now Spire Murrayfield Hospital, EH12 6UD). He broadened his scope to become a co-founder of the **Traverse Theatre Club** *Map p124* **M14** (now Traverse Theatre, now at 10 Cambridge Street, EH1 2ED) in 1963. Organized as a club to defeat censorship regulation, its aim was to present avant-garde and high-quality drama throughout the year, but especially to an international audience during the Edinburgh Festival. It opened in a tiny room in **James' Court** *Map p124* **P13** (493 Lawnmarket, Royal Mile, EH1 2PB), but soon built up a substantial reputation and moved to better premises.

Demarco also wanted to promote the visual arts, in particular to bring the work of little-known international artists, especially Eastern Europeans, to wider audiences. He championed artists such as Paul Neagu, Marina Abramovic and Joseph Beuys. There were overlaps with theatre, since some of the artists did performance art, and important theatre directors including Tadeusz Kantor were also invited. Most of the events and exhibitions took place at the **Demarco Gallery** *Map p120* **K13** (8 Melville Street, EH3 7NS and many other locations over the years), which was run as a not-for-profit venue in contrast to other parts of the festival. The purpose was to forge links with Europe and promote cultural dialogue. However, there was often controversy, with challenging 'stage happenings' that might include audience members co-opted as extras. One of Kantor's performances in 1972 was called the 'most talked-about event at the Edinburgh Festival'.

Often run on a shoestring, in its current incarnation the Demarco European Art Foundation has much more support. His extensive archives, about 10,000 documents covering Scottish cultural events from 1963 until the present, have been digitized and made available online. Demarco has been honoured in Poland, Italy and Britain for his promotion of the arts and enhancement of cultural life, having brought to Edinburgh many of the most important artists of the last fifty years.

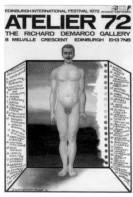

A poster from the Demarco Gallery, 1972 Edinburgh Festival (not on public display)

DOERS

∼ DOUGLAS, EARL HAIG ∼

1861–1928, SOLDIER

Douglas Haig was born at **24 Charlotte Square** Map p120 **L12** (carved in stone, to the right of no.24, above middle window, EH2 4ET), the youngest of eleven children of a wealthy whisky distiller (head of the family-run firm Haig and Haig) and his mother's favourite. He first went to school in St Andrews, then at the age of nine to the nearby **Edinburgh Collegiate School** Map p122 **M12** (27–28 Charlotte Square, EH2 4ET). Both parents died before he was eighteen.

He went to Brasenose College, Oxford, and lived with his brother's family at **42 Palmerston Place** Map p120 **J13** (EH12 5BJ) out of term time. He left without a degree and at first failed the entrance exams for the army's Staff College, but was later admitted. His poor record there and early slow start were to give way to a brilliant career. He went from being one of the oldest captains in the army to the youngest major-general in five years.

He became friends with the future Edward VII and in 1905 married the Hon. Dorothy Vivian, a lady-in-waiting to the Queen, in a chapel at Buckingham Palace. He was knighted in 1909. Having served in India, Egypt, Sudan and the Boer War, he was in charge of two divisions in France at the start of World War I, becoming Commander-in-Chief in 1915. His name is associated with heavy casualties, in particular on the Somme in 1916: 58,000 on the first day of battle. While he has been nicknamed Butcher Haig, he was little criticized during his lifetime.

After the war, he was created Earl Haig and helped to found the British Legion, with Poppy Day being his idea. The making of poppies became an employment for

Haig's dress uniform, Museum of Edinburgh Map p118 **T12**.

disabled ex-servicemen at **Lady Haig's Poppy Factory** Map p116 **O6** (9 Warriston Road, EH7 4HJ). At his death, his body lay in state at Westminster Abbey, then came by train to St Giles Cathedral, before being buried at Dryburgh Abbey. He is commemorated at the **National War Museum** Map p124 **N13** (Edinburgh Castle, Castlehill, equestrian statue in court; death mask and tunic within the museum, EH1 2NG), and there is a recreation of his field headquarters at the **Museum of Edinburgh** Map p118 **T12** (Huntly House, 142 Canongate, Royal Mile, also artefacts and portraits, second floor, EH8 8DD).

DOERS

GAVIN HASTINGS

1962–, RUGBY PLAYER

Andrew Gavin Hastings was born at **5 Old Kirk Road** (off map, EH12 6JY) then lived at **18 Merchiston Place** *Map p128* **K19** (EH10 4NS) and attended **George Watson's College** *Map p128* **J22** (22 Colinton Road, EH10 5EG), where he showed early promise when he was the first to captain a Scottish schoolboys' rugby team to win in England. He was also the all-time highest points scorer for his school. After study at Cambridge University, where he was also a star player, he went on to play rugby union for Scotland and for the British and Irish Lions. As a fullback, he played for Scotland a total of sixty-one times, twenty as captain. With the Lions, he has toured to Australia and New Zealand.

Hastings' first international match was against France in 1986. At this time he lived at **29 Alderbank Terrace** *Map p128* **F21** (EH11 1TA). Since then he has twice set a world record for most points scored in an international match, only for these records to have almost immediately been broken by another player in the same match. A member of the best-placing Scottish squad in the Rugby World Cup of 1991, he was also its highest point scorer until his record was superseded in 2007. By the time of his retirement, he had scored the third highest number of tries for Scotland of all time.

After retiring from rugby in 1996, Hastings played American football with the Scottish Claymores. Although not as successful as with his original sport, he was still part of the winning side in the World Bowl when they played at **Murrayfield Stadium** *Map p120* **D16** (EH12 5PJ).

Hastings has been called the greatest Scottish rugby player of all time. Known also for his ability to galvanize his team and build their confidence, he captained Scotland in one Rugby World Cup and played in two others. He is honoured in the Scottish Sports Hall of Fame in the **National Museum of Scotland** *Map p124* **Q14** (Chambers Street, 'Scottish Sports Hall of Fame', level 6, right of top of stairs, EH1 1JF). He and his family live in the Murrayfield area of Edinburgh.

DOERS

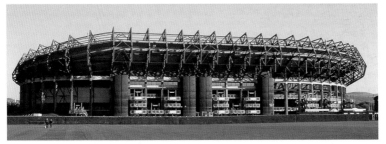

Murrayfield Stadium, where Gavin Hastings has often played rugby for Scotland *Map p120* **D16**.

～ HAMISH HENDERSON ～

1919–2002, FOLKLORIST AND POET

James Scott Henderson was born in Blairgowrie, the only son of a single mother. It is unclear whether he ever knew his father's identity. In 1928 they moved to Somerset, where his mother died when he was thirteen. The headmaster of his school then became his legal guardian. He wrote poetry and prose from a young age and could read and speak several languages. In 1938 he went to Downing College, Cambridge. He then enlisted and spent the war in North Africa and Italy, where he wrote widely disseminated songs and poetry. During this time, he also became a member of the Scottish National Party, with the idea of creating an independent socialist Scotland.

After a couple of visits to Scotland, he came to Edinburgh in 1946, where he met some of the leading poets, travelled and enjoyed Gaelic culture, but he never had a permanent home until he married in 1959. He did teacher training at **Moray House College of Education** Map p126 **S13** (St John Street, off Royal Mile, now part of the University of Edinburgh, EH8 8AQ), and was often penniless. In 1951 he founded the Edinburgh People's Festival, now considered the forerunner of the Fringe festival, with events at the **Oddfellows Hall** Map p124 **Q15** (now Malone's, 12–16 Forrest Road, EH1 2QN). He decided that the nearby **Sandy Bell's Bar** Map p124 **Q15** (25 Forrest Road, EH1 2QH) would be the fulcrum of his work. He was a hard drinker and could have a temper.

With his interests in traditional culture and music, he collected songs from groups such as traveller people and 'tinkers' and helped to found the **School of Scottish Studies** Map p124 **Q16** (University of Edinburgh, 27 George Square, EH8 9LD), where he continued to work almost until his death. His well-known song, *Freedom Come All Ye*, is viewed as the alternative Scottish national anthem, and his songs and poetry were influential during the

Scottish folk revival and internationally. His abiding passion was international peace, but he is best remembered as a poet, songwriter and folklorist. A bust of him is in the **National Museum of Scotland** Map p124 **Q14** (Chambers Street, 'Scotland, a Changing Nation', level 6, north-west section, EH1 1JF), and another at **Lochside Walkway** (off map, near Lochside Avenue, South Gyle, south-west of lochs, EH12 9DJ).

Sculpture of Hamish Henderson, Lochside Walkway, South Gyle (off map).

DOERS

SIR CHRIS HOY

1976–, CYCLIST

Christopher Andrew Hoy was born at **3 Wester Coates Terrace** *Map p120* **F14** (EH12 5LR) and attended **George Watson's College** *Map p128* **J22** (22 Colinton Road, EH10 5EG), where he competed in rugby and rowing. He became Scottish champion in BMX (bicycle motocross) at the age of fourteen and soon joined the City of Edinburgh Racing Club, training at **Meadowbank Velodrome** *Map p118* **Y10** (Meadowbank Sports Centre, 139–143 London Road, EH7 6AE). He went on to the University of St Andrews, then the **University of Edinburgh** *Map p124* **Q16** (George Square, EH8 9JX), where he graduated with a degree in applied sports science.

Concentrating on track cycling, Hoy's main events were initially the one-kilometre time trial and the team sprint. His first World Championship medal was in 1999 when he was part of the team in the latter event. Many others followed, with six Olympic gold medals, two Commonwealth titles and twenty-five World Championship gold, silver and bronze medals. After 2004, when the one-kilometre time trial was removed from the Olympics programme, he successfully switched his focus to compete in the keirin, an event in which for several laps a group of six to eight cyclists follow a motorbike which speeds up and then leaves the track, allowing a sprint to the finish line. In 2007 he tried to break the world record for one kilometre, but failed by only 0.005 of a second. He is the first Briton since 1908 to have won three gold medals in a single Olympics and the most successful Olympic cyclist of all time. His two gold medals at the 2012 London Olympics made him the most successful British Olympian of all time, with the most gold medals won. Some of his medals are in the **National Museum of Scotland** *Map p124* **Q14** (Chambers Street, entrance of 'Scottish Sports Hall of Fame', level 6, near stairs, EH1 1JF).

Hoy married lawyer Sarra Kemp at **St Giles Cathedral** *Map p124* **Q13** (Royal Mile, EH1 1RE) in 2010, and they now live in Salford, Greater Manchester, near the National Cycling Centre's velodrome. Besides cycling, he sometimes commentates on it for the BBC.

Hoy was named both Sportsman of the Year and Sports Personality of the Year in 2008, and he was knighted the following year.

Sir Chris Hoy's gold medal from the 2006 Commonwealth Games, National Museum of Scotland *Map p124* **Q14**.

~ JAMES VI AND I ~

1566–1625, ROYALTY

James was the only son of Mary, Queen of Scots, q.v., and Henry Stewart, Lord Darnley, q.v., born at **Edinburgh Castle** *Map p124* O13 (Royal Palace, Castlehill, cipher on ceiling of the Queen's Bedchamber, also portraits, EH1 2NG). His father was killed and his mother was forced to abdicate in the following year, making him King 'Jamie the Saxt' of Scotland at the age of one. He was raised a Protestant, with an education of 'censure and flattery', and learned several languages. He began to rule in his own right at the age of seventeen. As a youth he had shown great affection for a male cousin, but a marriage was arranged with the fourteen-year-old Anne of Denmark when James was twenty-three. The storms that raged during his journey to fetch her led him to believe that enemies were conspiring with witches to cast spells.

When Queen Elizabeth died in 1603 without a direct heir, James was at the **Palace of Holyroodhouse** *Map p118* **V12** (Canongate, Royal Mile, EH8 8DX). Although he had a good claim to the throne through both his parents, he learned that he would definitely succeed only when a messenger arrived. After a service at **St Giles Cathedral** *Map p124* Q13 (Royal Mile, EH1 1RE), he gave a farewell speech and borrowed money to get to London. He became the first monarch of a united Britain.

The scholarly James commissioned what is now called the King James Bible and wrote on various subjects, from *Daemonologie* on witchcraft to his well-known *Counterblast to Tobacco*. He survived assassination attempts and the Guy Fawkes plot. The king of France famously called him 'the wisest fool in Christendom'. He believed in the concept of a united Britain, extended royal authority to the Highlands and has been called a shrewd rather than creative ruler.

He returned to Edinburgh only once, in 1617, when festivities and banquets were prepared for him at the castle and at the **home of Baillie MacMorran** *Map p124* **P13** (Riddle's Court, 322 High Street, Royal Mile, plaque, EH1 2PG). Portraits are at Edinburgh Castle and the **Scottish National Portrait Gallery** *Map p122* **P10** (1 Queen Street, gallery 1, second floor, two portraits, miniature, EH21JD).

James's cipher, ceiling of the Queen's Bedchamber, Royal Palace, Edinburgh Castle *Map p124* O13.

~ SIR LUDOVIC KENNEDY ~

1919–2009, JOURNALIST

Ludovic Henry Coverley Kennedy was born at his grandparents' home at **4 Belgrave Crescent** Map p120 **J11** (EH4 3AQ). After attending Eton College, he enlisted as a naval officer soon after World War II broke out. His father, in command of HMS *Rawalpindi*, had already been killed.

After the war, he studied at Oxford and started his career as a journalist, in print and radio broadcasting. He became known for the issues he felt passionately about, in particular miscarriages of justice and the abolition of the death penalty. With his 1961 bestseller, *10 Rillington Place*, he successfully campaigned to overturn the conviction of Timothy Evans, hanged for the murder of his baby daughter in 1950, and helped to bring about the end of capital punishment. Another high-profile case was that of the Birmingham Six, jailed for terrorism, when he discussed the impact of police corruption. Other causes Kennedy championed were Scottish home rule, euthanasia and humanism.

Kennedy's career in journalism was nothing if not varied. He was especially well-known as a television newsreader and presenter, in particular on BBC's *Panorama* during the 1960s, which gave scope for airing the causes he supported. His television interviews and books were widely admired. However, he never took himself too seriously, appearing as himself in several episodes of the 1980s political satire series, *Yes, Minister*.

Because of his discrediting of aspects of the justice system and the police, Kennedy was not beloved of the establishment. He was blackballed for membership of a prestigious Edinburgh golf club. Prime Minister Margaret Thatcher refused to give him a knighthood, but he was honoured by John Major in 1994 for services to journalism.

Kennedy married dancer Moira Shearer, q.v., in 1950, and they lived at **3 Upper Dean Terrace** Map p120 **K10** (EH4 1NU), before moving to England in later years. He asked that after his death his ashes be scattered in the **Water of Leith** Map p116 **O6** (EH3 5LB), where he had played as a child, near his nephew's home in Warriston Crescent.

DOERS

~ TOM KITCHIN ~

1977–, CHEF

Thomas William Kitchin was born at **28 Barnton Park Avenue** (off map, EH4 6ES). He attended school in Scotland and went to catering school in Perth, before apprenticing at the prestigious Gleneagles Hotel. He served his cooking apprenticeship with several French chefs, who have all been awarded three Michelin stars, in top restaurants in London, Paris and Monte Carlo. Returning to Edinburgh, in 2006 he opened his own restaurant, inevitably called The Kitchin, at **78 Commercial Street** (off map, EH6 6LX), financing it with all his savings and a huge overdraft. Only six months later, at the age of twenty-nine, he became the youngest Scottish chef ever to win a Michelin star. Once the star had been awarded, waiting lists could be as long as eight weeks for a weekend booking. During this time he lived nearby at **12 Tower Place** (off map, EH6 7BZ) and then at **1 Liddesdale Place** *Map p116* **N7** (EH3 5JW).

In his 2009 book, *From Nature to Plate*, Kitchin outlined his cooking philosophy: to use seasonal Scottish ingredients, coupled with classic French techniques. This straightforward approach has won him numerous awards, with a best UK restaurant accolade in 2010 from both the *Observer Food Monthly* and *Square Meal* guide. In the same year he opened a second restaurant, Castle Terrace, at **33–35 Castle Terrace** *Map p124* **N14** (EH1 2EL). Run by chef Dominic Jack, it operates with the same approach to food as its sister enterprise. A third restaurant opened in 2013.

Media appearances have included being a guest judge and mentor on *MasterChef*, in which aspiring chefs try to impress with their recipes and cooking skills, followed by giving work experience to its 2010 winner, Dhruv Baker, at The Kitchin. In 2008 he had also competed against other top chefs on the *Great British Menu*, becoming the Scottish winner.

Kitchin runs his restaurant with his wife, Michaela Berselius. The noted chef Albert

Roux is reported to have said that Kitchin is the most likely Scottish chef to win the full three stars from Michelin.

The Kitchin, Tom Kitchin's Leith restaurant (off map).

DOERS

ERIC LIDDELL
1902–45, ATHLETE

Henry Eric Liddell was born near Beijing, China, the second son of Scottish missionaries from Edinburgh. His forenames were quickly reversed when his father realized the initials were unfortunate. Sent to school in England, from a young age he excelled at cricket, rugby and athletics. He went on to the University of Edinburgh in 1920, staying briefly at **21 Gillespie Crescent** *Map p128* **M17** (EH10 4HU) and **4 Merchiston Place** *Map p128* **L19** (EH10 4NR) with his family, and then between 1922 and 1924 at the **Edinburgh Medical Missionary Society Hostel** *Map p126* **R16** (56 George Square, now part of the University of Edinburgh, plaque, EH8 9JU). He attended the **Morningside Congregational Church** *Map p128* **L20** (15 Chamberlain Road, since demolished, Morningside United Church on same site, EH10 4DJ).

From 1921 he triumphed in every race he ever ran in Scotland, won medals and broke records, in 1923 setting a new British record for the 100 yards. One of the places he trained was the **Powderhall Stadium** *Map p116* **P5** (Powderhall Road, since demolished, EH7 4GB). He also played for the Scotland rugby team, scoring ten tries in his first two matches. But he is most remembered for refusing to compete in the preliminary heats at the 1924 Paris Olympics, since they took place on a Sunday. The 1981 film, *Chariots of Fire*, told the story. He still won a bronze and a gold, and set a new world record for the 400 metres.

He graduated in 1924 with a BSc, then studied for a year at the **Scottish Congregational College** *Map p128* **O20** (29 Hope Terrace, EH9 2AP) before returning to missionary work in China. He married Florence McKenzie in 1934. In 1941, when pregnant with her third daughter, she took their children to Canada to avoid internment by the Japanese. However, Liddell was himself interned in 1943 and died in the camp of a brain tumour.

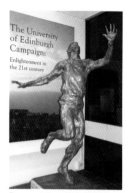

Known as the Flying Scotsman, he is commemorated at the **Eric Liddell Centre** *Map p128* **L20** (15 Morningside Road, EH10 4DP), the **University of Edinburgh** *Map p126* **R14** (Old College, South Bridge, left side, University Offices, statue; and through glass doors, through doors back left, display case on left with Olympic medals, EH8 9YL) and the **National Museum of Scotland** *Map p124* **Q14** (Chambers Street, 'Scottish Sports Hall of Fame', level 6, right of top of stairs, EH1 1JF). Locations used for *Chariots of Fire* include the **Café Royal** *Map p122* **Q11** (19 West Register Street, EH2 2AA) and **Broughton McDonald Church** *Map p118* **R9** (33 Broughton Place (as the Church of Scotland, Paris), now Lyon & Turnbull, EH1 3RR). A 2008 poll in *The Scotsman* newspaper voted him the most popular athlete Scotland has ever produced.

Bronze statue of Eric Liddell, showing his unique running style, University of Edinburgh, Old College *Map p126* **R14**.

DOERS

CHRYSTAL MACMILLAN

1872–1937, SUFFRAGIST

Jessie Chrystal Macmillan was born at **8 Duke Street** Map p118 **V4** (since demolished, now former railway station, EH6 8HQ), the family soon moving to **2 Belford Park** Map p120 **H13** (EH4 3DP). She was an only daughter with eight brothers. After school in Edinburgh and St Andrews, she was the first woman to graduate in science at the **University of Edinburgh** Map p126 **R14** (Old College, South Bridge, EH8 9YL) in 1896.

Her mother had died in 1894, and she had the unenviable task of taking care of her father, eight brothers and a large household at **Corstorphine Hill House** (off map, now within Edinburgh Zoo, Members' House of the Zoological Society, 134 Corstorphine Road, EH12 6TS) where they now lived. Her great cause was women's suffrage, for which she campaigned tirelessly, working with Elsie Inglis, q.v., and speaking all over Scotland. She was the second woman to plead before the House of Lords in 1908, when she argued, albeit unsuccessfully, that women graduates should be allowed to vote. In 1909 she took part in a large march for women's rights held along **Princes Street** Map p122 **N12** (EH2 3AA).

Macmillan went to London in about 1912 to carry on the fight on issues such as equal rights for women in the workplace and the welfare of prostitutes. It was also a more prominent place to campaign for women's suffrage. In 1918 women over thirty were granted the vote, something she and her colleagues could be proud of. Also a peace campaigner, she was a delegate to the Paris Peace Conference of 1919. She fought for many other aspects of women's rights as well, for example that a woman's nationality should be independent of that of her husband. She qualified as a lawyer in 1924, only the fourth woman in England to do so.

When she suffered a thrombosis and had to have a leg amputated in 1937, she returned to Edinburgh, where she died at **8 Chalmers Crescent** Map p128 **Q19** (EH9 1TR). She is commemorated with a plaque at the **University of Edinburgh** (off map, King's Buildings, West Mains Road, turn off road, first left, Joseph Black Building on right, plaque right of entrance, EH9 3JJ)

Chrystal Macmillan Building, University of Edinburgh, George Square Map p124 **Q16**.

and a university building, the **Chrystal Macmillan Building** Map p124 **Q16** (15a George Square, EH8 9LD). Her name is on her parents' tombstone at **Corstorphine Old Parish Church** (off map, 2a Corstorphine High Street, through Kirk Loan gates, right of path, largest monument (Celtic cross), EH12 7ST).

DOERS

Queen Margaret

C.1045–93, ROYALTY

Margaret was born in Hungary, the granddaughter of the English king, Edmund Ironside. She and her family came to England in 1057, but following the Norman Conquest they were returning to Hungary in 1067, possibly having stopped in Northumbria, when their ship was blown off course. They landed at what is now called St Margaret's Hope, west of what became North Queensferry, and sought the protection of the king. Malcolm III married Margaret three years later. He was probably a widower and about forty-five, and she about twenty-four.

Margaret was educated and read English and Latin, while Malcolm was illiterate. She introduced English fashions to the court and was also renowned for her charitable acts, notably her custom of inviting nine orphans to breakfast. A devout woman, she wanted to unify the church in Scotland and so changed the language of the mass from Gaelic to Latin and in general worked for the dominance of the Roman Church over the Celtic Church. When the Western Isles became subject to Malcolm's rule, they went to Iona to rebuild the abbey. She created the ferries at what are now North and South Queensferry to facilitate the journeys of pilgrims on their way to Dunfermline Abbey and St Andrews.

In later life, Malcolm and Margaret lived at **Edinburgh Castle** Map p124 O13 (Royal Palace, Castlehill, EH1 2NG). Malcolm and her eldest son were killed in battle in 1093 and she died three days later, possibly of anorexia due to fasting. She was the mother of eight children, with three of her sons becoming kings of Scotland. One of them, David, built **St Margaret's Chapel** Map p124 O13 (Castlehill, EH1 2NG) in her honour in about 1100.

Because of her piety, reported miracles and good deeds, Margaret was canonized in 1250, and is now revered in both the Catholic and Anglican churches. She is commemorated with murals at the **Scottish National Portrait Gallery** Map p122 P10 (1 Queen Street, Touchscreen Gallery, first floor, EH2 1JD), and Queen Margaret University is named for her.

DOERS

Queen Margaret's Chapel, Edinburgh Castle
Map p124 O13.

MARY QUEEN OF SCOTS

1542–87, ROYALTY

Mary was born at Linlithgow Palace, but was taken to France at the age of six to escape the political upheavals of the time, coming back to Scotland only at the age of nineteen, when she began her reign. It lasted for only six years, during which time she lived at the **Palace of Holyroodhouse** Map p118 **V12** (Queen's Outer Chamber, second floor, Canongate, Royal Mile, embroideries, other artefacts, EH8 8DX).

She was married three times, to Francis II of France, Lord Darnley, q.v., and the Earl of Bothwell. Her only child was James, the future James VI of Scotland and James I of England, q.v., son of Darnley, born at **Edinburgh Castle** Map p124 **O13** (Royal Palace, Castlehill; her coronation crown and the crown jewels, bust and portrait, also on view, EH1 2NG). She was a tall, beautiful and well-educated woman, a linguist, musician and horse-rider. Men considered her charming and vivacious, and she enjoyed their company. After the death of Francis in 1560, she returned to Scotland in 1561, arriving at Leith and resting at **Lamb's House** Map p118 **V2** (corner of Water Street and Burgess Street, since demolished, seventeenth-century house on same site, EH6 6SU). She was married to Darnley for only eighteen months before he was killed in mysterious circumstances. The Earl of Bothwell immediately divorced his wife and married her.

A Catholic, she inevitably clashed with her Protestant cousin Queen Elizabeth and the supporters of the Scottish Reformation, in particular, John Knox, q.v. To the French and other Catholics, Mary was the rightful queen of England, as Elizabeth was the daughter of an illegitimate marriage. Despite the fact that Mary did not interfere with the Protestant Church in Scotland, plots were laid against her. But her real crime to the

A Catte, one of many embroideries by Mary Queen of Scots, Palace of Holyroodhouse. It is thought Mary saw herself as a mouse and Queen Elizabeth as a large ginger cat Map p118 **V12**.

general public was her supposed adultery, unacceptable in a woman. Her reign collapsed, as she had alienated almost every part of society, and she was taken prisoner in 1567, spending her last night at the **home of the Lord Provost** Map p124 **Q13** (the lodgings of Sir Simon Preston of Craigmillar, since demolished, plaque at City Chambers, 253 High Street, Royal Mile, EH1 1YJ). She escaped but was recaptured and spent the rest of her life in prison, plotting to overthrow Elizabeth. She was beheaded as a traitor. Portraits and a bust are in the **Scottish National Portrait Gallery** Map p122 **P10** (1 Queen Street, library, first floor, medallion, bust; gallery 1, second floor, two portraits, EH2 1JD).

～ JOHN MENZIES ～

1808–79, BOOKSELLER

John Menzies, pronounced 'ming-is' in Scotland, was born in Edinburgh and apprenticed to a bookseller in Regent Road. He went to London in 1830 to work in Fleet Street, where he made good contacts, but had to return to Edinburgh when his father died three years later. He started his own business at **61 Princes Street** Map p122 O12 (now renumbered as 76 Princes Street, near north-east corner with Hanover Street, jeweller's, EH2 2DF) that same year. There he made many innovations which helped his business to expand. He began to sell *The Scotsman* newspaper, previously available only if delivered by the publisher to people's homes; he inaugurated bookstalls at **Waverley Station** Map p122 Q12 (Waverley Bridge, EH1 1BB) and other Scottish railway stations; he became a wholesaler to the book trade; and he published books and engravings. He supplemented the usual stock for a bookshop to include many stationery items, such as pens and account books. Early to recognize the talent of Charles Dickens, he acquired the sole rights to sell his work in the east of Scotland and also became the sole Scottish agent for *Punch* magazine. Very much the Victorian gentleman, he vowed 'not [to] sell any book objectionable in its moral character or tendency'.

When he married in 1845, he moved to **16 Scotland Street** Map p122 P9 (EH3 6PX) and later to **28 Nelson Street** Map p122 O9 (EH3 6LJ), with his last address **3 Grosvenor Crescent** Map p120 J14 (EH12 5EP). He is buried at **Warriston Cemetery** Map p116 O4 (42 Warriston Gardens, through gates, along path and down slope, fifth path on left, bear left, first right, middle of row on left, EH3 5NE).

The business continued to expand after his death, with his sons and partners carrying on his legacy. Still trading over a hundred years later, the flagship bookshop was at **107 Princes Street** Map p122 N12 (now Next shop, EH2 3AA), with more than a hundred shop assistants by the 1990s, but its retail stores were sold to rivals W. H. Smith in 1998. Today the headquarters of John Menzies plc are at **108 Princes Street** Map p122 N12 (EH2 3AA), with former offices at **Hanover Buildings** Map p122 O12 (56–58 Rose Street, shop sign, EH2 2YQ),

both very near the original bookshop. The successful multinational company distributes around 45 per cent of Britain's newspapers and magazines to retailers and is the world's leading aviation services business.

The old John Menzies shop sign at 56–58 Rose Street
Map p122 O12.

DOERS

~ YVONNE MURRAY ~

1964–, ATHLETE

Yvonne Carol Grace Murray was born in Musselburgh, where her father was a joiner. The family lived at **1a Moir Drive** (off map, Musselburgh EH21 8EF) and then at **6 Galt Road** (off map, Musselburgh, EH21 8DJ). At **Musselburgh Grammar School** (off map, 86 Inveresk Road, EH21 7BA) she was playing hockey when one of the teachers spotted her and thought she would make a runner. She started to train by running on roads on the outskirts of Musselburgh and on the path beside the nearby River Esk, doing five one-mile repetitions at a time, interspersed with short breaks. Conditioning and track work took place at Meadowbank Stadium, where she also competed with the Edinburgh Athletic Club. At sixteen she won the 3,000-metre race at the British Schools competition held in Dublin, setting a new record. Since that time she has concentrated on middle- and long-distance track and road-running events, mainly the 3,000- and 10,000-metre races.

Murray was chosen to compete for Scotland in the 1982 Brisbane Commonwealth Games, where she finished tenth, but she reached peak form at the following one, held in 1986 in Edinburgh. Running at her home ground of **Meadowbank Stadium** Map p118 **Y10** (Meadowbank Sports Centre, 139–143 London Road, EH7 6AE), she won bronze for the 3,000 metres. At the 1988 Olympics, held in Seoul, she won another bronze medal, following that with gold for the 3,000 metres at the 1990 European Championships and at the 1993 World Indoor Championships. At the 1994 Commonwealth Games, running the 10,000 metres, she won another gold. She has twice been British champion at 3,000 metres and once at 5,000 metres.

As one of Scotland's most successful athletes of the 1980s and 1990s, Murray was

awarded an MBE in 1990 and named BBC Scotland Sports Personality of the Year in 1994. She is honoured in the Scottish Sports Hall of Fame at the **National Museum of Scotland** Map p124 **Q14** (Chambers Street, 'Scottish Sports Hall of Fame', level 6, right of top of stairs, EH1 1JF) and in the **Scottish National Portrait Gallery** collection Map p122 **P10** (1 Queen Street, not on display, EH2 1JD). Now retired from running, Murray works as an athletics development and events officer in Lanarkshire, often with aspiring athletes.

Postcard and photo collage of Yvonne Murray, by David Mach, Scottish National Portrait Gallery (not on display).

～ SIR MALCOLM RIFKIND ～

1946–, POLITICIAN

Malcolm Leslie Rifkind was born at **29 Morningside Road** *Map p128* **L21** (EH10 4DR) to a Jewish family who had been immigrants from Lithuania in the 1890s. Educated at **George Watson's College** *Map p128* **J22** (22 Colinton Road, EH10 5EG) and the **University of Edinburgh** *Map p126* **R14** (Old College, South Bridge, EH8 9YL), he studied law, then did a post-graduate degree in political science. After a short time as a university lecturer in Rhodesia, now Zimbabwe, he prac-tised as an advocate, during which time he was also a local councillor for **Edinburgh Town Council** *Map p124* **Q13** (now Edinburgh City Council, City Chambers, 253 High Street, Royal Mile, EH1 1YJ). From 1974 he repre-sented Edinburgh Pentlands as its Conservative MP, while living with his family at **1 Drummond Place** *Map p122* **P9** (EH3 6PH).

During the Conservative reign of eighteen years, Rifkind was one of only four min-isters to serve the entire time. He initially supported the introduction of Margaret Thatcher's poll tax in Scotland, but later accepted that it had been a terrible mistake. He was also sometimes at odds with his party over their policies against devolution for Scotland. His final two posts were as Defence Secretary and Foreign Secretary. In the former office, he opposed British involvement in the Bosnian war in the mid-1990s, in conflict with American views. In the latter, he committed the British government for the first time to a Palestinian state. However, in common with all Conservative MPs in Scotland and Wales, he lost his seat in 1997 when Labour won with a landslide. He was knighted in the resignation honours list.

While he has since been in tune with most of the Conservative Party's poli-cies, he broke ranks and criticized Tony Blair's, q.v., support for the invasion of Iraq in 2003. In 2005 he was elected as MP for the London seat of Kensington and Chelsea. A senior figure in his party, he also campaigns on issues he feels strongly about, including support for the Global Zero movement, which works toward the elimination of nuclear weap-ons. Another cause is the revitalization of the Commonwealth. He makes his views known through frequent media appearances.

The City Chambers of Edinburgh City Council, Royal Mile *Map p124* **Q13**.

∽ THOMAS TELFORD ∽

1757–1834, ENGINEER

Thomas Telford was born in rural Dumfriesshire. His father, a shepherd, died soon after he was born, and his impoverished mother brought him up alone. He apprenticed as a stonemason at the age of fifteen before going to Edinburgh in 1779. While studying architecture and civil engineering, he laboured building **Princes Street** Map p122 **N12** (EH2 3AA) and the New Town. He also improved his architectural drawing skills by sketching at places such as **Rosslyn Chapel** (off map, Chapel Loan, Roslin, EH25 9PU). In 1782 he left for England, where he worked on numerous projects for new roads, bridges, canals and harbours.

His major work in Edinburgh was the **Dean Bridge** Map p120 **K11** (Queensferry Road, plaque in centre, EH4 3AS), built in 1830–31 over a deep ravine of the Water of Leith, one of the highest bridges in the world when it was constructed. It allowed new land to be developed for housing north-west of the city centre.

Telford has been called the greatest Scottish engineer of his time. Within Scotland, he supervised the building of the Caledonian Canal, which helped to open up the Highlands and the north. Many Scottish harbours were also built or improved, as well as 120 new bridges and about 1,500 kilometres of roads.

The majority of his work took place in England, primarily Shropshire, but he also advised the king of Sweden on the building of a canal. Other achievements include the building of the Menai Suspension Bridge in Wales, the longest suspension bridge of its day; and the Galton Bridge in the West Midlands, the longest single span bridge at the time.

Telford died in London and was buried in Westminster Abbey. He is commemorated

at the **National Museum of Scotland** Map p124 **Q14** (Chambers Street, 'Shaping our World', level 5, plans, EH1 1JF). He helped to establish the profession of civil engineering and left a huge legacy in the built environment, most of which is still in use today.

Dean Bridge from the Water of Leith
Map p120 **K11**.

DOERS

∼ Lord Thomson of Fleet ∼

1894–1976, NEWSPAPER AND MEDIA OWNER

Roy Herbert Thomson was born in Toronto, the son of a barber of Scottish ancestry. After working his way through business school, he had a number of jobs, one of which was selling radios in northern Ontario. Business was poor since there were no stations to listen to, so Thomson bought a radio frequency and transmitter, first broadcasting in 1931. He gradually shifted from selling radios to concentrating on the radio station, before widening his scope to buy a small-town newspaper in 1934 and subsequently many other businesses. In 1952 he moved to Edinburgh and bought the majority shareholding in **The Scotsman** newspaper *Map p122* Q12 (now The Scotsman Hotel, 20 North Bridge, EH1 1TR) the following year. He revitalized the paper through reorganization and an injection of capital, but didn't seek editorial control, later saying '...editorial content, that's the stuff you separate the ads with'. In 1957 he bought one of the first commercial television franchises, which became Scottish Television, famously saying it was his 'licence to print money'.

He went on to buy the *Edinburgh Evening News*, the city's other main paper, but one that covers local issues. He expanded his media empire to include the *Sunday Times* group, saving it from ruin, eventually owning over 200 newspapers in Canada, the USA and Britain, more than anyone else at the time, as well as other businesses under the umbrella of the multinational Thomson Organization. Interests ranged from North Sea oil to the travel company, Thomson Holidays.

In 1964 he was ennobled with the hereditary title of Baron Thomson of Fleet, having to renounce his Canadian citizenship to do so. His Edinburgh home was at **22 Braid Avenue** (off map, EH10 6EE), but he was not welcomed into Edinburgh society and was hurt by the snub. Never ostentatious, he travelled by tube when in London, which is where he died. His legacy is the Thomson Corporation, one of the largest information enterprises in the world.

The former offices of *The Scotsman*, now a hotel, North Bridge *Map p122* Q12.

6

THE UNCATEGORIZABLE

The most saintly, the most dastardly and the most eccentric don't easily fit into categories, so one has had to be devised for them. Their lives and deeds may make your hair stand on end. You will find out about famous criminals, the murderers Burke and Hare and the Jekyll-and-Hyde character, Deacon Brodie, inspirations for many a film and work of fiction. Burke and Hare supplied a steady stream of corpses for Dr Robert Knox's anatomy lessons, no questions asked. Knox was not quite a criminal but was at least an accessory. On the edge of the world of crime was Dora Noyce, who kept the most respectable brothel in town. Her friend, Madame Doubtfire, a seller of smelly second-hand clothing, was the inspiration for a novel, which became a classic film starring Robin Williams.

On the other side of the criminal divide are two members of the police force. The Victorian detective James McLevy wrote about real cases he had dealt with, inspiring at second hand Arthur Conan Doyle. More recently William Merrilees adopted disguises and detection techniques worthy of Sherlock Holmes to catch miscreants and even a German spy.

In earlier times, Lord Darnley, the husband of Mary Queen of Scots, was a tempestuous man and a murderer, whose rages and jealousies may have led to his own death at the age of twenty-one. Two young women, Jessie King and Margaret Dickson, were hanged in Edinburgh. King had killed at least one baby, but Dickson's crime was only the concealment of a pregnancy. By arrangement with the hangman or by a miracle, she survived and became famous as Half-Hangit Maggie.

Miracles, or at least miraculous poems, were attributed to two other women, Agnes McLehose and the Venerable Margaret Sinclair. Sinclair, born in the slums of Edinburgh, is on the first step of the ladder to canonization. Agnes McLehose, known as Clarinda, inspired Robert Burns to write magical poetry.

In some cases, little is known about the lives of those mentioned. James Miranda Barry was a woman who disguised herself as a man so that she could go to medical school and practise as a doctor. No wonder she hid the facts about her identity. John Edmonstone, born a slave, taught Charles Darwin taxidermy, but his life was hardly recorded, since he was only a lowly bird-stuffer. At the other end of the spectrum, Peter Williamson wrote about and publicized his life story, which may or may not have been entirely truthful.

Two well-known animals are connected to Edinburgh – Greyfriars Bobby and Dolly the sheep. Again, the story of Bobby is unlikely to be as Walt Disney told it, but Dolly was real and her stuffed remains are available for all to see.

Some of the uncategorizable had lives that sound like tall tales, ones that you couldn't make up. They include the best and the worst, the privileged and the unfortunate, all part of the light and the dark sides of Edinburgh.

The tea cup that reputedly belonged to Clarinda, the muse of Robbie Burns, National Museum of Scotland
Map p124 **Q14**.

~ JAMES MIRANDA BARRY ~

C.1789–1865, DOCTOR

While there are different versions of Barry's life, the most likely story is that she was born Margaret Ann Bulkley in Ireland. The family was in financial distress, with her father in prison, so they decided to send her to medical school to get them out of debt. She took the name of her uncle, the painter James Barry, who had died in 1806 and whose legacy would fund her studies. She added that of the Venezuelan revolutionary General Francisco de Miranda, who, with his extensive library, had helped her to prepare for university. He and others in their London circle had liberal, even radical ideas, which included the then-unthinkable, that a woman could qualify as a doctor. Dressed as a young man, she travelled with her mother to Edinburgh in 1809, arriving by sea. Despite being only five feet tall and delicate in appearance, she was able to carry off the deception.

As James Barry, she took up her studies at the **University of Edinburgh** Map p126 **R14** (Old College, South Bridge, plaque north-west corner, EH8 9YL), gaining her medical doctorate in 1812. Returning to London, she enrolled at the United Hospitals of Guy's and St Thomas and in 1813 passed her examinations and became a member of the Royal College of Surgeons.

Still maintaining her masculine identity, Barry now joined the British Army as a hospital assistant, serving in India, South Africa and many other places. In South Africa, she performed one of the first successful Caesarean sections. A strong but sometimes difficult personality, she rose to Inspector General but got into trouble and was demoted, eventually rising again to the same position. Her empathy led her to fight for better conditions for soldiers, prisoners and lepers.

When she died of dysentery, one report was that she was discovered to be a woman. Others maintain that she or he was a hermaphrodite. If female, she was the first woman medical doctor in Britain and the first woman graduate of the University of Edinburgh.

The plaque at the University of Edinburgh commemorating James Miranda Barry Map p126 **R14.**

~ DEACON BRODIE ~

1741–88, CABINET-MAKER AND CRIMINAL

William Brodie was born in **Brodie's Close** *Map p124* **P13** (304 Lawnmarket, Royal Mile, EH1 2PS), the only son of a cabinet-maker. He joined the family business in 1780 and soon became a respected craftsman, rising quickly in his craft guild to be appointed a deacon, or senior official, and serving as a town councillor. However, he also enjoyed gambling, drinking and his mistresses. His favourite haunts included James Clarke's Tavern in **Fleshmarket Close** *Map p124* **Q13** (199 High Street, off Royal Mile, EH1 1QA) and the Cape Club in **Craig's Close** *Map p124* **Q13** (middle of south side of Cockburn Street, plaque, EH1 1BN), where he tried to better his luck by using loaded dice. He turned to crime in about 1786, needing to support these habits and his mistresses' children. He copied customers' keys while he worked on their premises, returning later to rob them.

Mr BRODIE

With his partners in crime, he embarked on what was to be his most daring heist in 1787. They broke into the Excise Office (tax office) at **Chessel's Court** *Map p126* **S13** (240 Canongate, Royal Mile, EH8 8AD), but missed the £600 hidden in the cashier's secret drawer and got away with only £16. When the crime was discovered, one of his partners was captured and turned king's evidence. Brodie's house was searched. The burglar's tools found there incriminated him, and he fled first to England and then to Amsterdam, where he was apprehended when about to embark for America, traced through letters sent to his mistress.

Model of Deacon Brodie, Brodie's Close, Royal Mile *Map p124* **P13**.

Brodie was returned to Edinburgh, where he was tried and sentenced to hang in the **Lawnmarket** *Map p124* **P13** (Royal Mile, near south-east corner of George IV Bridge, three brass markers in street, EH1 1RF), by some accounts on the gallows he had himself designed. He was buried in an unmarked grave at **Buccleuch Parish Church** *Map p126* **R16** (not signposted, now derelict, west side of Chapel Street, EH8 9AY). His double life – respectable citizen by day and criminal by night – inspired Robert Louis Stevenson, q.v., to write *The Strange Case of Dr Jekyll and Mr Hyde*. Furniture made by him or his father can be seen at the **Writers' Museum** *Map p124* **P13** (Lady Stair's Close, Lawnmarket, off Royal Mile, cabinet made by Brodie that had been in Robert Louis Stevenson's bedroom, EH1 2PA) and the **National Museum of Scotland** *Map p124* **Q14** (Chambers Street, 'Scotland Transformed', level 3, middle, mahogany cabinet by father of Deacon Brodie, EH1 1JF), and his portrait by John Kay, q.v., is in the **Scottish National Portrait Gallery** *Map p122* **P10** (1 Queen Street, gallery 7, second floor, print, EH2 1JD).

⁓ BURKE AND HARE ⁓

WILLIAM BURKE, 1792–1829, CRIMINAL
WILLIAM HARE, 1792 OR 1804–C.1858–60, CRIMINAL

William Burke and William Hare were Irish labourers who came to Edinburgh to work on the construction of the Union Canal. Hare lived in a lodging house with the widowed proprietor in **Tanner's Close** Map p124 **N14** (since demolished, near north-east corner of Lady Lawson Street and West Port, EH3 9DR), and Burke and his wife later moved in. When another lodger died owing rent, Hare asked Burke to help him take the corpse to **Surgeons' Square** Map p126 **R14** (High School Yards, now part of University of Edinburgh, bear right and through archway, EH1 1LZ), where it was known that bodies were always needed for anatomy lessons. A student directed them to Dr Robert Knox's, q.v., rooms. They were asked no questions, paid £7/10s and requested to supply more.

'Resurrection men' often dug up newly buried bodies for this grisly trade, but Burke and Hare thought that too much trouble. They determined instead to take the easier route of finding people no one would miss, mostly the old, poor, female and infirm. They would ply them with drink before smothering them. Between 1827 and 1828 they killed about sixteen people. The last victim, Marjory Docherty, was murdered in a close in the **West Port** Map p124 **O14** (EH1 2LF). This final killing was traced back to the two men.

Hare gained immunity from prosecution by turning king's evidence and was released in 1829. By some accounts he died about thirty years later, a pauper in London. Burke was hanged in the **Lawnmarket** Map p124 **P13** (Royal Mile, near south-east corner of George IV Bridge, three brass markers in street, EH1 1RF), watched by a huge crowd. As was the custom, his body was publicly dissected at the **Edinburgh Medical College** Map p126 **R14** (now University of Edinburgh, Old College, South Bridge, EH8 9YL). His death mask and a pocket book made from his skin are in the **Surgeons' Hall Museum** Map p126 **R14** (18 Nicolson Street, EH8 9DW), his skeleton is at the **Anatomical Museum** Map p124 **Q15** (Old Medical School, Teviot Place, EH8 9AG) of the university, and life masks of both men are at the **Scottish National Portrait Gallery** Map p122 **P10** (1 Queen Street, library, first floor, EH2 1JD). A broadsheet about the execution is in the **National Museum of Scotland** Map p124 **Q14** (Chambers Street, 'Scotland Transformed', level 3, middle, EH1 1JF). The pair have been the subject of many films, the most recent a comedy, *Burke and Hare*, 2010. Locations included **Merchant Street** Map p124 **P14** (EH1 2QD) and **Old Fishmarket Close** Map p124 **Q13** (190 High Street, Royal Mile, EH1 1RW).

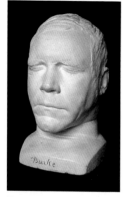

The death mask of William Burke, Surgeons' Hall Museum Map p126 **R14**.

CLARINDA

C.1759–1841, MUSE

'Clarinda' was born Agnes Craig, the daughter of a Glasgow surgeon. At the age of seventeen she married a lawyer, James McLehose, but left him after four years because of his violence. In 1782 she and her children moved to Edinburgh where she took rooms in **Potterrow** Map p126 **R15** (General Entry, Potterrow, since demolished, plaque at north-east corner of Potterrow and Marshall Street, EH8 9BL). She was determined to meet the poet Robert Burns, q.v., when he arrived in Edinburgh for the second time in 1787. Her friend Miss Nimmo invited them both to tea at her house in nearby **Alison Square** Map p126 **R15** (since demolished, now Marshall Street at Potterrow, south side, EH8 9BT). They were besotted with each other, but because Burns had an accident which meant he was housebound for six weeks, they began an impassioned and lengthy correspondence, with up to six letters each a day. They met a second time at Miss Nimmo's while he was still injured.

Because she was still a married woman, she and Burns called themselves Clarinda and Sylvander in case their letters went astray. Her maid, Jenny Clow, was charged with delivering them, and Peter Williamson's, q.v., runners brought Burns's replies to her. While Clarinda's relationship with Burns was likely chaste, Jenny bore him a son in November 1788.

In 1791 Clarinda decided to try to save her marriage. She met Burns for the third and last time at the **White Hart Inn** Map p124 **O14** (34 Grassmarket, EH1 2JU). His famous song, *Ae Fond Kiss*, was written for her at this time. Early in 1792, she sailed from Leith for Jamaica where her husband now lived, but upon arrival she found that he had taken up with a local woman, so she quickly returned to Edinburgh. From 1800 until her death, she lived in a flat at **14 Calton Hill** Map p118 **R11** (since demolished, north side, off Regent Road, EH1 3BJ). She is buried at the **Canongate Kirk** Map p118 **T12** (153 Canongate, Royal Mile, east wall, right side of church, EH8 8BN), and artefacts are in the **Writers' Museum** Map p124 **P13** (Lady Stair's Close, Lawnmarket, off Royal Mile, silhouette and poem, EH1 2PA) and the **National Museum of Scotland** Map p124 **Q14** (Chambers Street, level 5, south, cup and saucer said to have belonged to her, EH1 1JF).

She was considered a great beauty and had a 'spirit unusually gay, frank, and emotional'. At his death, Burns was still carrying her silhouette.

Poem by Clarinda, *On the Autumn of Life*, Writers' Museum Map p124 **P13**.

Henry Stewart or Stuart, first Duke of Albany, and later known as Lord Darnley, was born in Yorkshire. His royal connections were through several routes, in particular his mother, a sister of Henry VIII. This also made him the first cousin of Mary Queen of Scots, q.v.

A highly ambitious man, he flirted with Queen Elizabeth, but she sent him to Scotland to her cousin Mary. He danced seductively with her, and Mary became infatuated with him, calling him 'the lustiest and best pro-portionit man'. The nineteen-year-old became her second husband in 1565, when they married in a Catholic cer-emony at the **Palace of Holyroodhouse** Map p118 **V12** (Canongate, Royal Mile, EH8 8DX).

From the start it was a marriage of convenience, furthering Darnley's ambitions, since he was now King Consort of Scotland, but also Mary's. Darnley's ancestry would strengthen both her and her heirs' claims to the English throne. However, although Darnley was outwardly attractive, he was also weak, pathologically jealous and given to violence. With accomplices, he murdered Mary's secretary, David Rizzio, in front of her, thinking he was the father of her unborn child, the future James VI and I, q.v.

Darnley was becoming an embarrassment to Mary and the court, for example by betraying confidential information. In 1567 he was convalescing from smallpox at the house of **Kirk o' Fields** Map p126 **R14** (since demolished, site of Old College, University of Edinburgh, South Bridge, EH8 9YL). Mary often stayed in the room below, but had left before explosives put there razed the house. Darnley and his servant were later found **nearby in a field** Map p126 **R14** (outside the town wall, now South College Street, EH8 9AA), unharmed by the blast but strangled.

Suspicion immediately fell on the Earl of Bothwell, Mary's next husband, who was tried but not convicted. The crime has never been solved. However, it is possible that Darnley himself put the explosives in Mary's room, so that he could suc-ceed, but was strangled by courtiers who had discovered his plot. He was buried at **Holyrood Abbey** Map p118 **V12** (back wall, right-hand side, Canongate, Royal Mile, access through Palace of Holyroodhouse, EH8 8DX) and his por-trait is in the **Scottish National Portrait Gallery** Map p122 **P10** (1 Queen Street, gallery 1, second floor, EH2 1JD).

The cipher of Darnley and Mary Queen of Scots (M for Mary and A for Duke of Albany), Edinburgh Castle, entrance to the Royal Palace Map p124 **O13** (Castlehill, EH1 2NG).

THE UNCATEGORIZABLE

MARGARET DICKSON

C.1705–?60, 'HALF-HANGIT MAGGIE'

Margaret Dickson was born about 1705, probably near Edinburgh. As a young woman she was a fishwife in Musselburgh. In 1723, when she was about eighteen, her husband deserted her and she went to work at a Kelso inn in the Scottish Borders. She became pregnant by the landlord's son, but concealed her condition, fearing the loss of her job and lodgings. Her baby was either stillborn or died shortly after birth. She hid the body on the banks of the Tweed, where it was discovered and she was soon traced. Concealing a pregnancy was in itself a crime, so it was not a matter of whether she had killed the baby. When a woman did not seek help with the birth and the child was missing or dead, it was equivalent to murder and so carried the death penalty. Maggie was arrested and sent for trial in Edinburgh. She was quickly found guilty and sentenced to be hanged in September 1724 in the **Grassmarket** Map p124 **P14** (site of the gallows, north-east part of Grassmarket, EH1 2JR). Once the sentence had been carried out and the hangman had pulled on her legs to ensure she was dead, her body was taken down, to be carried to Inveresk churchyard. On the way, the mourners rested, and passing workmen alerted them to noises coming from the coffin. When the lid was opened, Maggie sat up. After a few days, she was fully recovered and had become a celebrity.

Under Scots Law, she was considered dead and was therefore free. It was God's will that she had survived. Another possibility is that she had offered sexual favours to the

hangman to provide a looser knot. With her new fame as Half-Hangit Maggie, her husband resurfaced and remarried her, and she gave birth to a son only nine or ten months after the hanging. She lived for up to forty more years, working either as a salt-seller or an innkeeper. **Maggie Dickson's Pub** Map p124 **P14** (92 Grassmarket, EH1 2JR) commemorates her name.

The shadow of the gallows, now immortalized in the paving of the Grassmarket Map p124 **P14**.

⌒ DOLLY THE SHEEP ⌒

1996–2003, CLONED MAMMAL

Dolly the sheep was the first mammal to be cloned from the cell of an adult of the same species. She had three 'mothers'. One provided the egg, a second the DNA and a third, space in her womb to carry her to term. Sir Ian Wilmut, Keith Campbell and colleagues developed the cloning technique at the **Roslin Institute** (off map, now the Roslin Biotechnology Centre, Roslin, EH25 9TT) near Edinburgh. A cell taken from the mammary gland of an adult sheep was the basis for the clone. After 277 attempts, Dolly was the first lamb to survive into adulthood. She owes her name to the fact that the scientists were impressed by the mammary glands of the country singer, Dolly Parton. She had a normal life for a sheep and gave birth to six (uncloned) lambs.

While it was a scientific breakthrough to create Dolly, its ethics have been questioned, in particular since Dolly died prematurely. However, it has not been possible to state definitively whether her death was the result of premature ageing as the result of the cloning or just bad luck. A sheep normally lives for about twelve years, while Dolly was only six when she died of a form of lung cancer that is relatively common in sheep that live indoors. She also had severe arthritis from the age of four. It is possible that the age of a cloned animal should be calculated as a combination of the age of its donor at the time of cloning plus its own age.

Dolly may be seen at the **National Museum of Scotland** Map p124 **Q14** (Chambers Street, 'Connect' Gallery, level 1, EH1 1JF), and a cast of her head and photos are at the **Scottish National Portrait Gallery** Map p122 **P10** (1 Queen Street, gallery 11, first floor, plaster and scrim cast of her head, four photos, EH2 1JD). Undoubtedly the world's most famous sheep, she heralded a new age in which it may be possible to clone even extinct animals. However, controversy still surrounds the issue, especially in regard to the cloning of humans.

MADAME DOUBTFIRE

1887–1979, SHOPKEEPER

Annabella Cruickshank Adams was born in Aberdeen. At eighteen she married Arthur Doubtfire, a London-born bugler with the Scottish Rifles. He was killed during World War I, and in 1917 she made her way to Edinburgh, taking up residence at **1 and 3 South East Circus Place** Map p122 **N10** (now Doubtfire Gallery, EH3 6TJ), where she set herself up as a pawnbroker. When a signwriter suggested having 'Madame' instead of 'Mrs' Doubtfire on her shop front, she readily agreed.

She scandalously took up with James Coutts from Dundee, a married man five years her junior. They were living together in her premises in 1921 when his wife conveniently died, and they married only two weeks later. Coutts disappeared from the scene at some later stage, but Madame Doubtfire ran her shop from the same address for sixty years.

In the 1980s, the author Anne Fine was living nearby at **73 Dundas Street** Map p122 **O9** (top flat, EH3 6RS), writing a novel about a father whose former wife blocks access to their children. He solves the problem by dressing as a nanny and getting the job of taking care of them. Fine called her eponymous character Madame Doubtfire, just because she had visited the shop and liked the name. The novel was turned into the 1993 film, *Mrs Doubtfire*, starring Robin Williams. It had the same premise as the book, but the story was much revised to show off the cross-dressing talents of its star and has become a classic.

In later years, Madame Doubtfire was selling smelly second-hand clothing and living with many cats in the back of the shop. A cantankerous woman, she sat outside her north-facing door in all weathers, often knitting mismatched socks and smoking a clay pipe. When she became infirm, she went to **Greenlea's Old People's Home** (off map, now flats, now 17 The Steils, EH10 5XD) where she greatly enjoyed regaling the other residents with her stories. She died at **Longmore Hospital** Map p128 **T19** (now Historic Scotland, Salisbury Place, EH9 1SH), aged ninety-one. She would have been amazed at her international posthumous fame.

Madame Doubtfire's former shop is now a gallery using her name Map p122 **N10**.

THE UNCATEGORIZABLE

JOHN EDMONSTONE

TAXIDERMIST, C.1790–?1843

John Edmonstone was born a slave, probably in Demerara, now in Guyana, South America, where his Scottish owner, Charles Edmonstone, ran a sugar plantation. The owner's son-in-law taught John taxidermy. Charles brought him to the family home in Glasgow in about 1817 and, once on British soil, he was no longer a slave; a ruling in England in 1772 and confirmed in Scotland a few years later meant that any slave who came to Britain was now free. He left his former master's service and moved to Edinburgh, living first at **37 Lothian Street** Map p124 **Q14** (since demolished, EH1 1HB) in 1824, and then from 1825 at **51 Lothian Street** Map p124 **Q15** (since demolished, EH1 1HB), where he taught taxidermy to students at the University of Edinburgh, including Charles Darwin, who lived with his brother Erasmus along the road at **11 Lothian Street** Map p124 **Q14** (since demolished, plaque on museum, EH1 1HE). Darwin called him a 'pleasant and intelligent man' and, besides taxidermy, learned about the South American rainforests from him. He thought Edmonstone's fees were a bargain. 'He only charges one guinea, for an hour every day for two months.' These lessons proved invaluable during Darwin's voyages, and he also came to abhor slavery after hearing the first-hand accounts.

Edmonstone also found employment as a 'bird-stuffer', one of two listed in the Post Office directories of the time, by selling items to the **Royal Museum of the University** Map p124 **Q14** (now the Talbot Rice Gallery, University of Edinburgh, Old College, South Bridge, EH8 9YL). He lived at several addresses in Edinburgh over a twenty-year period, including at **6 South St David Street** Map p122 **P11** (since demolished, side of Jenner's department store, EH2 2YJ), and **10 South St David Street** Map p122 **P11** (since demolished, side of Jenner's department store, EH2 2YJ) the last address he is listed at in the directories in 1843. It is not known what happened to him after this time.

It is possible that Edmonstone inspired the young Darwin to travel to South America and its Galapagos Islands, where he started to put together his theory of evolution and change the way we understand human and animal development.

An *aracari*, a bird like a toucan, of the type John Edmonstone provided to the predecessor of the National Museum of Scotland Map p124 **Q14**.

GREYFRIARS BOBBY

C.1855–C.67 AND C.1865–72, LOYAL DOG

There are two main versions of the life of Greyfriars Bobby, neither of which is likely to be true. An American author, Eleanor Atkinson, who had never visited Scotland, wrote the best-known version in 1912. In it, Bobby refused for fourteen years to leave the graveside of his master, John Gray, a shepherd who had died while attending a market. Another researcher cast doubt on the story, but found a policeman of the same name buried at Greyfriars and said that Bobby was a police dog. However, a ten-inch-high Skye terrier is suitable for neither role.

The more likely story is that Bobby was a stray who had wandered into the grounds of the neighbouring **Heriot's Hospital** *Map p124* **P15** (now George Heriot's School, Lauriston Place, EH3 9EQ), and had been thrown over the gate to **Greyfriars Kirkyard** *Map p124* **P14** (1 Greyfriars Place, EH1 2QQ) by the

Greyfriars Bobby's collar with his licence, Museum of Edinburgh *Map p118* **T12**.

gardener in about 1858. He was still an illegal resident, but when the newspapers took up the story of a loyal dog, the cemetery warden profited by selling postcards and getting tips from the many visitors, eager to know about him. He became so valuable to him and to John Traill, the owner of the nearby **Temperance Coffee House** *Map p124* **Q14** (now computer shop, 6 Greyfriars Place, EH1 2QQ), that when he died in about 1867, another dog was substituted. The first dog was a terrier cross, the second a pure-bred Skye terrier.

From 1867, Bobby was a celebrity. He would take his cue from the one o'clock gun fired from **Edinburgh Castle** *Map p124* **O13** (Castlehill, Royal Mile, EH1 2NG) to go for lunch at Traill's. Many other people befriended him, so that he didn't have to sleep outside, but he enjoyed ratting at the cemetery. The Lord Provost paid for his licence, in recognition of his loyalty. His collar is in the **Museum of Edinburgh** *Map p118* **T12** (Huntly House, 142 Canongate, Royal Mile, first floor, EH8 8DD), and his statue at **George IV Bridge** *Map p124* **P14** (corner of George IV Bridge and Candlemaker Row, EH1 1EN). A grave marker is at the entrance to Greyfriars Kirkyard, and the grave of PC John Gray nearby. Whatever the true story, Greyfriars Bobby is still admired and even beloved.

∽ Jessie King ∽

1862–89, CRIMINAL

Jessie King or Kean was probably born in or near Edinburgh. She and her much older partner, Thomas Pearson, first lived at **24 Dalkeith Road** *Map p128* **U18** (EH16 5BS), where they used a number of aliases. As Mr and Mrs Macpherson, they moved to **Ann's Court, Canonmills** *Map p116* **O7** (since demolished, east of middle of Canon Street, near petrol station, EH3 5HE), and set up the business of what was then called baby farming. Unmarried mothers would pay for the long-term fostering of their babies, since it was socially impossible to keep them. Baby farming was a legal but shameful solution to a Victorian problem, when poor single mothers had few options.

One boy in King's care, Alexander Gunn, suddenly disappeared, but she moved to **Cheyne Street** *Map p120* **K9** (east side, EH4 1JA) before suspicion could fall on her. There a girl, Violet Thompson, also went missing. When some boys found the body of a strangled baby boy nearby, she was questioned by the police. She broke down and led them to the cellar where she had hidden the girl's body. King was charged with the two murders and tried for the murder of the boy.

In the High Court, King claimed that 'drunken melancholy' had made her strangle the boy and that she had accidentally given the girl too much whisky, trying to get her to sleep. She was inevitably found guilty and sentenced to be hanged. Thomas Pearson claimed to have known nothing about the disappearances of the children, saying unconvincingly that he thought they had gone elsewhere.

King was examined by prominent doctors Henry Littlejohn, q.v., and Joseph Bell, q.v., and a medical commission pronounced her sane. She went calmly to her death, the last woman hanged in Edinburgh, and was buried at **Calton Prison** *Map p118* **R11** (since demolished, now site of St Andrew's House, 2 Regent Road, EH1 3DG) under what is now the west car park. The hangman was reported to have said that 'he never saw a woman meet her death so bravely'. It is possible she killed other babies, and she also had a child of her own, whose fate is unknown.

Part of the wall of the now-demolished Calton Prison *Map p118* **R11**.

THE UNCATEGORIZABLE

∼ Dr Robert Knox ∼

1791–1862, ANATOMIST

Robert Knox was the son of a schoolmaster in Edinburgh. He attended **Edinburgh Medical College** *Map p126* **R14** (now University of Edinburgh, Old College, South Bridge, EH8 9YL) and qualified as a doctor in 1814, before a few years as an army surgeon. He returned to Edinburgh in 1822, when he set himself up as a freelance lecturer in anatomy at **10 Surgeons' Square** *Map p126* **R14** (High School Yards, now Chisholm House, part of University of Edinburgh, bear right and through archway, EH1 1LZ). Medical students could choose who taught them, and Knox was one of the most popular because he was an inspired lecturer and also able to demonstrate dissection and surgical techniques on fresh corpses. Other lecturers relied on the standard practice of preserving bodies and using them again and again.

Bodies for medical science were in short supply, since the only ones available were those of hanged criminals. Body snatchers would dig up newly buried bodies to sell to Knox and other doctors, an illegal but lucrative trade. Then the notorious Burke and Hare, q.v., had the idea of murdering down-and-outs for the purpose. Knox and his assistants paid well and asked no questions.

Once Burke had been executed in 1829, however, Knox was vilified. At the hanging, the crowd shouted, 'Hang Knox! Hang noxious Knox!' Sir Walter Scott, q.v., who witnessed the event, accused him of 'trading deep in human flesh'. A mob attacked his

A recreation of Robert Knox's room at Surgeons' Square, Surgeons' Hall Museum *Map p126* **R14**.

home at **4 Newington Road** *Map p128* **T18** (now re-numbered as 17 Newington Road, EH9 1QR) and hanged him in effigy, while he escaped out the back door. He was not charged with murder, but the authorities found he had acted incautiously. His reputation suffered, he had few students and got into debt. Ironically, the Anatomy Act of 1832, for which he had campaigned, allowed freer access to bodies, so that he lost his advantage over other lecturers. He eventually left for London in 1842. He was buried in an unmarked grave in Woking.

Despite the unsavoury trade he engaged in, he was responsible for advances in knowledge of anatomy and for the training of many successful surgeons. He is commemorated at the **Surgeons' Hall Museum** *Map p126* **R14** (18 Nicolson Street, tableau, EH8 9DW).

THE UNCATEGORIZABLE

∼ James McLevy ∼

c.1800–73, Police Detective and Writer

James McLevy or McLeive was born in County Armagh, Ireland, and spent four years as an apprentice weaver. He came to Edinburgh aged about nineteen, where he worked as a labourer, before becoming a nightwatchman for the Edinburgh police in 1830. In 1833, while ill at the **Royal Infirmary** Map p126 **R14** (now School of GeoSciences, University of Edinburgh, Drummond Street, EH8 9XP), he reported a nurse who had been stealing his wine. When discharged from hospital, he resigned from his job on doctor's orders, but was instead promoted to become a detective, the first in the Edinburgh police force to deal with criminal cases. He lived initially at **Old Flesh Market Close** Map p124 **Q13** (now Fleshmarket Close, 199 High Street, off Royal Mile, EH1 1QA) and later in the **Canongate** Map p126 **R13** (1 Mint, beside 242 Canongate, now South Gray Close, 40 High Street, off Royal Mile, EH1 1TQ) first with his wife, then his sister, then a female servant.

He dealt with thousands of cases over his career, almost always securing a conviction, and when he retired he wrote about them in three books of stories, the first of which was published in about 1861. He described in detail the seamy underbelly of Edinburgh, both the criminal and the unfortunate. Besides explaining his detection techniques, he expressed his compassion for those such as the 'chance-begotten brats, squalling with hunger, or lying dead for days after they should have been buried'. His work was plagiarized by W. C. Honeyman, writing under the pseudonym James McGovan. Arthur Conan Doyle, q.v., came across these latter stories. McLevy's methods are similar to those of Conan Doyle's detective, Sherlock Holmes, although McLevy described actual events rather than fictional ones. Because of the popularity of his stories, he became so famous that he was consulted by parliament and advised on dealing with convicts.

McLevy was living at **South Richmond Street** Map p126 **S15** (now east part of West Richmond Street, EH8 9DZ) when he died and was buried at the **Canongate Kirk** Map p118 **T12** (153 Canongate, Royal Mile, unmarked grave, near that of Francis Marshall, enclosure with red chippings, west side of church towards back of cemetery, EH8 8BN). Many of his stories have been adapted and serialized on BBC Radio 4, set mainly in Leith and featuring his characters Jean Brash, a madam, and a real colleague, Constable William Mulholland.

~ William Merrilees ~

1898–1984, POLICEMAN

William Merrilees was born at **Cochrane's Pend** *Map p118* **V3** (44 Kirkgate, Leith, since demolished, near supermarket, EH6 6AD), one of eight children. The family soon moved to a two-roomed flat at **91 St Andrew's Street** *Map p118* **V2** (since demolished, now 91 Giles Street, Leith, EH6 6BZ), where there was no running water. He was sent to work at the age of eight, before full-time employment at thirteen at a rope works. In an industrial accident there he lost all the fingers of his left hand. Apparently accident-prone, he was frequently in **Leith Hospital** *Map p118* **T2** (8–10 Mill Lane, now closed, EH6 6TJ), but he was also an excellent swimmer and saved seventeen people from drowning.

His life-saving brought him to the attention of the Lord Provost, who recommended him to the police force, although at 5'6" he was four inches below the minimum height requirement and had an imperfect left hand. An exception was made, and he was appointed a constable in 1924.

Merrilees became known as a latter-day Sherlock Holmes for his inspired detective work and mastery of disguises. His small stature meant that he was able to masquerade as a baby in a pram, when nannies were being threatened by a molester. His most famous coup was the apprehension of a German spy, Werner Walti, at **Waverley Station** *Map p122* **Q12** (Waverley Bridge, EH1 1BB) during World War II. Disguised as a railway porter, he overpowered Walti before he could draw his pistol.

By 1950 he had risen to become Chief Constable of the Lothians and Peebles Constabulary, with his office at **302–310 Lawnmarket** *Map p124* **Q13** (Police Chambers, now renumbered as 192a High Street, Royal Mile, now coffee shop, EH1 1RF). From about this time he lived at **41 Park Road** (off map, EH6 4LA). He retired on his seventieth birthday, long past the normal age.

Always remembering his early life in poverty, Merrilees was renowned for his charitable work, whether dressed as Father Christmas for visits to children's homes, helping the children of offenders or giving free swimming lessons. He also believed in cautioning prostitutes and trying to find them alternative employment, rather than the prevalent harsh treatment. 'Wee Willie' is remembered both for his big heart and his crime-solving abilities.

The former Police Chambers, where William Merrilees was Chief Constable, now a coffee shop, Royal Mile *Map p124* **Q13**.

THE UNCATEGORIZABLE

~ DORA NOYCE ~

1900–77, BROTHEL KEEPER

Georgie Hunter Rae was born at **196 Rose Street** and also lived as a child at another address in the same street *Map p122* **M12** *and* **N12** (196 near numbers 194 and 198, EH2 4AT; and 126 Rose Street, since demolished, near shoe shop, EH2 3DT), at the time notorious for prostitution. She worked in the sex trade herself, although she called herself a housekeeper, and began to use the name Dora. When she gave birth to a daughter in 1923, at **23 Cowan's Close** *Map p126* **S16** (since demolished, near EH8 9HF), she also started to use the surname of the child's father, Ernest Noyce.

From around the end of World War II, she ran a brothel, or what she called a house of leisure and pleasure, at **17 Danube Street** *Map p120* **K10** (EH4 1NN), in an elegant and upmarket Georgian terrace. Apart from the fact she was the proprietor of a house of ill repute, she was the ultimate in respectability. She was well-spoken, wore a fur coat and twin set and supported the Conservative Party, putting posters in her windows during election campaigns. She owned property at **22 Hamilton Place** *Map p120* **L9** (EH3 5AU), other parts of Edinburgh and in Blackpool. However, she also appeared at the **Sheriff Court** *Map p124* **P13** (now High Court of Justiciary, Lawnmarket, Royal Mile, north-east corner with Bank Street, EH1 2NT) for living off immoral earnings, where she was fined forty-seven times and also served a four-month sentence in 1972.

Noyce employed about fifteen sex workers, with twenty-five more on call for busy periods. She claimed her best custom was during the Edinburgh Festival, but second best was the General Assembly of the Church of Scotland, its annual conference. American and other sailors were also frequent customers, sometimes queuing round the block. She claimed she was offering a necessary social service. The brothel operated until her death, but for years afterwards the new owners were plagued with drunken punters demanding entry at all hours.

A well-known local character and friend of another one, Madame Doubtfire, q.v., Noyce is remembered for her business acumen, but also for her grace under pressure. It is claimed that when the police once raided the place, she calmly asked, 'Business or pleasure, gentlemen?'

Number 17 is the blue door in the elegant Georgian terrace of Danube Street *Map p120* **K10**.

THE VENERABLE MARGARET SINCLAIR

1900–25, NUN

Margaret Ann Sinclair was born to an impoverished family living in a slum basement flat at **24 Middle Arthur Place** *Map p126* **S14** (since demolished, approximate site Briery Bauks, EH8 9TE), the third of six children of Andrew, a dustman, and his wife Elizabeth. The devoutly Catholic family had her baptized at the nearby St Patrick's Church. Shortly after, they moved to **13 Blackfriars Street** *Map p126* **R13** (EH1 1NB), where Sinclair attended **St Anne's Roman Catholic School** *Map p126* **R13** (now St Anne's Community Centre, 40 High Street, 6 South Gray's Close, EH1 1TQ). She had to leave school at fourteen and went to work as a French polisher at the **Waverley Cabinet Works** *Map p126* **R13** (17 South Gray's Close, 40 High Street, since demolished, near EH1 1TE) until its closure in 1918, then worked at the McVitie and Price Factory, which made biscuits. During this time she was an active member of her trade union. At the same time she attended evening classes at the **Edinburgh School of Cookery and Domestic Economy** *Map p120* **K14** (forerunner of Queen Margaret University, 3 Atholl Crescent, EH3 8ET), where she took certificates in domestic subjects.

Wishing to become a nun, she applied to a convent in the Liberton area of Edinburgh, but with no vacancy there they advised her to try the Poor Clare convent in London. She was accepted there in 1923 and, once 'clothed' in her nun's habit in 1924, took the name of Sister Mary Francis of the Five Wounds. By early 1925, however, she was suffering from tuberculosis and died later that year in a sanatorium. She was buried in north London, before being reinterred in 1927 at Mount Vernon cemetery, Liberton, and eventually at St Patrick's Church in 2003.

The shrine commemorating the Venerable Margaret Sinclair, St Patrick's Church *Map p126* **R13**.

In 1978 Pope Paul VI declared her Venerable, the first step in the process of canonization, following apparent miracles experienced by people who had prayed to her. One of them occurred when the two-year-old Jimmy Savile, who later became a media personality, recovered from a fall after his mother had prayed to her photograph at Leeds Cathedral. Besides her grave, there is also a museum dedicated to her memory at **St Patrick's Church** *Map p126* **R13** (5 South Gray's Close, 40 High Street, grave and shrine in north-west of church, museum with artefacts in south-east, EH1 1TQ).

PETER WILLIAMSON

1730–99, ADVENTURER AND WRITER

Born at Aboyne, the son of a ploughman, the thirteen-year-old Peter Williamson was kidnapped at nearby Aberdeen and transported to Philadelphia. The ship's captain sold his indentures to a Scots farmer there for about £16, saying he owned them. Before the seven years of service were over, the kindly owner had died, leaving Williamson £150 and his best horse.

In 1854 Williamson was able to marry and set up as a farmer on land given to him by his father-in-law, but shortly afterwards he was captured by the Delaware tribe. He was tortured, then escaped and joined the American army to fight in the Seven Years' War. His wife had died in the interim. He was again captured, this time by the French, and was returned to England with other soldiers in exchange for French prisoners.

Now destitute, he earned money by styling himself Indian Peter, dressing in costume and telling his tale or performing 'Indian' war whoops. He came to Edinburgh in about 1758, where he lodged at **James' Court** Map p124 **P13** (493 Lawnmarket, Royal Mile, EH1 2PB). When he opened a coffee house in Parliament Square and a tavern in **Old Parliament Close** Map p124 **Q13** (since demolished, east side of St Giles Cathedral, Royal Mile, EH1 1RE), he put a wooden Indian outside it. He had published a book about his adventures in America, *French and Indian Cruelty*, possibly exaggerated or even partly fabricated. In 1763 he raised a court action against the Aberdeen worthies who had allowed and profited from his kidnapping, winning £100 in damages and exposing a scandal.

With the money he set up a printing business at the **Luckenbooths** Map p124 **Q13**

(since demolished, middle of the Royal Mile near St Giles Cathedral, EH1 1RE) in 1773 and published the first street directory for Edinburgh, which continued annually until 1796. In 1774 he started the Williamson Penny Post service with seventeen shops as sub-post offices, including his own premises at **Swan's Close** Map p124 **Q13** (since demolished, between Anchor Close and Geddes Close, near 241 High Street, Royal Mile, EH1 1PE). Letters were delivered by his runners every hour within a mile radius of the Mercat Cross. He was buried in his Indian costume at the **Old Calton Burial Ground** Map p118 **R11** (Waterloo Place, north-east section, unmarked grave fifteen paces north-east of the Martyrs' monument (huge obelisk), with a memorial to another Williamson, possibly related, EH1 3EG).

James' Court, where Peter Williamson first lived when he came to Edinburgh
Map p124 **P13**.

THE UNCATEGORIZABLE

EDINBURGH
CELEBRITY CITY GUIDE

For each of the hundred celebrities, you can find the locations associated with them by using the seven colour-coded maps. Locations include where they lived, went to school or worked, where a statue or their grave is or where artefacts associated with them are housed. Check the celebrity's page, then the grid reference on the relevant map. Some of the people have locations on several different maps. Or if you will be visiting a particular site, for example, the Scottish National Portrait Gallery or the Writers' Museum, pages 132–138 show which of the celebrities have artefacts or images there. In some cases there is merely an association, for example if it is a theatre where the celebrity performed.

see pp116-117

Inverle

INVER

see pp120-121

QUEENSFERRY RD

Dean Cemetery

DEAN VILLAG

Modern Two
(formerly the
Dean Gallery)

Modern One
(formerly the Scottish
National Gallery
of Modern Art)

Water of Leith

Haymarket
Station

HAYMARKET

Murrayfield
Stadium

see pp128–129

Tynecastle
Stadium

George
Watson's
College

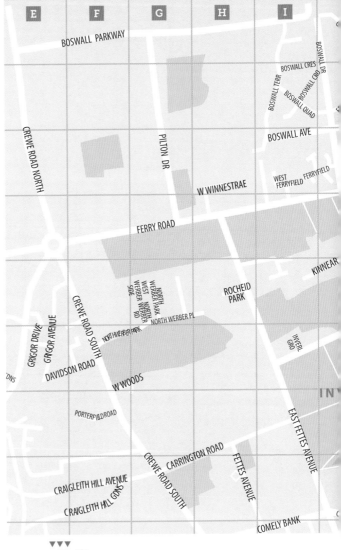

▼ ▼ ▼
see pp120–121

Robert Louis Stevenson q.v. said of Edinburgh, 'It was what Paris ought to be. It has a scenic quality that would best set off a life of unthinking, open-air diversion.'

John Buchan, the author of *The Thirty-Nine Steps*, said that Edinburgh had made more history than any town its size except Athens, Jerusalem or Rome.

Modern Art Two, formerly the Dean Gallery, was originally an orphanage founded in 1830 by Louis Cauvin, who also taught French to Robert Burns, q.v.

In 1645 the University of Edinburgh temporarily decamped to Linlithgow, so that staff and students would be safe from the plague.

▼▼▼
see pp122-23

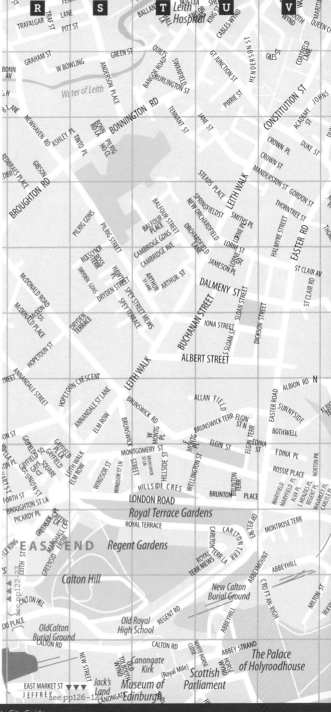

The Edinburgh Festival is the world's largest arts festival, held in August. During that time the size of the city doubles its normal population of about half a million. It attracts over a million visitors a year, making it the second most visited city in Britain after London. Its most popular attraction is Edinburgh Castle.

Edinburgh is said to be built on seven hills, although which seven is a matter of opinion. Two of them are extinct volcanoes – Castle Rock, the site of Edinburgh Castle, and Arthur's Seat, within Holyrood Park. A climb to the top of either is rewarded with panoramic views.

Prince Charles has said that Edinburgh is, 'In my estimation the most beautiful city in Britain', while the poet John Betjeman thought it 'the most beautiful of all the capitals of Europe'.

More than 300 witches were burned at the stake near the Castle Esplanade, Castlehill before the law was changed in 1736. A memorial to them designed by Sir Patrick Geddes, q.v., the Witches Well, is a tribute to these unfortunate women.

The Heart of Midlothian is heart-shaped granite setts in the paving just west of St Giles Cathedral. It is the site of the doorway to the Old Tolbooth gaol, built in the 15th century and demolished in 1817. Condemned prisoners would leave the Tolbooth for the short walk west to the gallows at the Lawnmarket, marked in the paving with brass.

Among the founding fathers of the Royal Society of Edinburgh in 1783 were Adam Smith, q.v., Joseph Black, q.v., James Hutton, q.v. and the American polymath, Benjamin Franklin. In 1771 Franklin had stayed with David Hume, q.v. for a month.

see pp122-23

see pp124-125

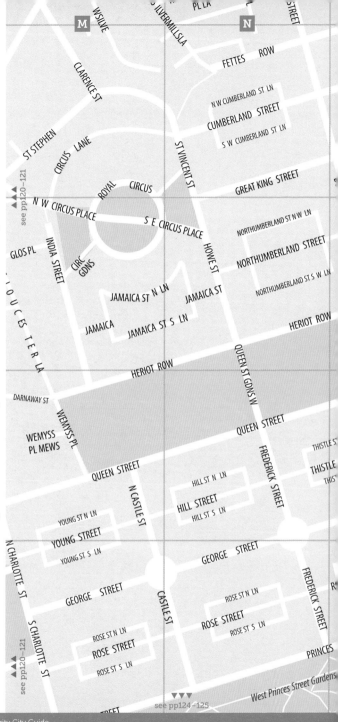

see pp120–121
see pp120–121
see pp124–125

see pp124–125

M

see pp122

N

West Gardens Cottage

West Princes Street Gardens

PRINCES S

National War Museum

Edinburgh Castle

see pp120–121

LOTHIAN ROAD

KING'S STABLES RD

CASTLE TERR

Traverse Theatre

CAMBRIDGE ST

CORNWALL ST

KING'S STABLES RD

KING'S STABLES

Usher Hall

Royal Lyceum Theatre

GRINDLAY ST

GRINDLAY ST LN

SPITTAL ST

WEST PORT

LADY LAWSON ST

LOTHIAN ROAD

BREAD ST

EAST FOUNTAINBRIDGE

LAURISTON ST

SEMPLE ST

RIEGO ST

HIGH RIGGS

LAURISTON PL

EARL GREY ST

DUNBAR ST

LAURISTON PK

LAURISTON GDNS

GLEN ST

PONTON ST

TOLLCROSS

W TOLLCROSS

THORNYBAUK

HOME ST

BROUGHAM ST

LAURISTON PL

PANMURE PL

LONSDALE TERR

DRUMDRYAN ST

BROUGHAM PL

see pp120–121

TARVIT ST

LEVEN TERR

GILMORE PLACE

see pp128–129

VALLEYFIELD

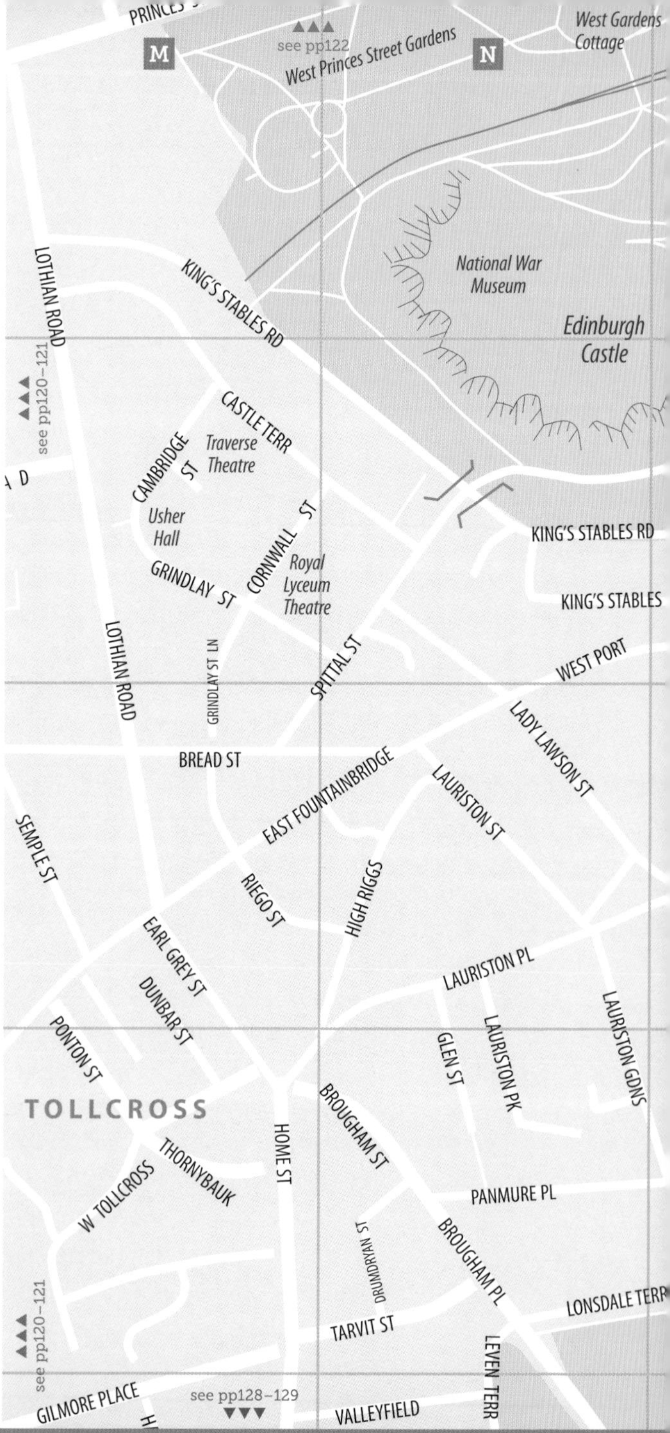

MARKET ST

see pp123

P

COCKBURN ST

Q

FLESHMARKET CLOSE

CRAIG'S CLOSE

SOUTH B

N BANK ST

ST. GILES ST

WARRISTON'S CLOSE

City
Chambers

HIGH STREET

MOUND PL

The Writers'
Museum

(Royal Mile)

13

RAMSAY GDNS

JAMES' COURT

RAMSAY LN

LAWNMARKET (Royal Mile)

St Giles Cathedral

PARLIAMENT SQ

OLD FISHMARKET CLOSE

BLAIR

CASTLEHILL

CASTLE
SPLANADE

UPPER
BOW

GEORGE IV BRIDGE

VICTORIA ST

W
BOW

COWGATE

GUTHRIE ST

MERCHANT ST

CANDLEMAKER ROW

CHAMBERS ST

WEST COLLEGE ST

14

GRASSMARKET

HERIOT BRIDGE

GREYFRIARS PL

National
Museum
of Scotland

BRIGHTON ST

LOTHIAN ST

see pp126–127

V
E
N
N
E
L

Greyfriars
Kirkyard

BRISTO PL

rgh
ge
rt

KEIR ST

HERIOT PL

George Heriot's
School

FORREST RD

TEVIOT PL

Old Medical
School

BRISTO SQ

15

LES ST

LAURISTON PL

LAURISTON PL

University
of Edinburgh

ARCHIBALD
PL

LAURISTON
TERR

CHARLES ST LA

NIGHTINGALE WAY

GEORGE

CHALMERS STREET

SIMPSON LOAN

GEORGE SQUARE

LAURISTON

SQUARE

16

MEADOW LANE

0   200m

The Meadows

see pp128–129

0   1/4 mile

R (Royal Mile)

S

CARRUBBER'S
PAISLEY CLOSE
BLACKFRIARS ST
S GRAYS CLOSE
NIDDRY ST
ST MARYS ST
ST JOHN ST
Gullan's Cl
Boyd's Entry

SMITH BRIDGE

COWGATE

HOLYROOD RD

VIEWCRAIG GARDENS

HIGH SCH YDS

ST JOHNS HILL

INFIRMARY

Surgeons' Square

PLEASANCE

DRUMMOND ST

ROXBURGH ST

ROXBURGH PL

W ADAM ST

NEW ARTHUR PL

NEW ARTHUR ST

BRIERY BAUKS

VIEWCRAIG GARDENS

University
Edinburgh
College
EGE ST

Surgeons'
Hall
Museums

RICHMOND PL

Festival
Theatre

see pp124

NICOLSON ST

HILL PL

NICOLSON SQ

MARSHALL ST

BROWN ST

WEST RICHMOND ST

RICHMOND LA

DAVIE ST

PLEASANCE

CARNEGIE ST

GILMOUR ST

WEST NICOLSON ST

NICOLSON ST

HADDON'S CL

HOWDEN ST

HARDWELL CL

ST LEONARD'S ST

BEAUMONT PL

CHAPEL ST

QUARRY CL

NDMILL ST
WINDMILL LN

W CROSSCAUSEWAY

E CROSSCAUSEWAY

COWANS CL

NEW JOHNS PL

FORBES LA

Former
Buccleuch
Parish Church

BUCCLEUCH ST

CLERK ST

EUCH PL

BUCCLEUCH PL LN

MEADOW LANE

SOUTHSIDE

RANKEILLOR ST

ST LEO

see pp128–129

GIFFORD PK

MONTAGUE ST

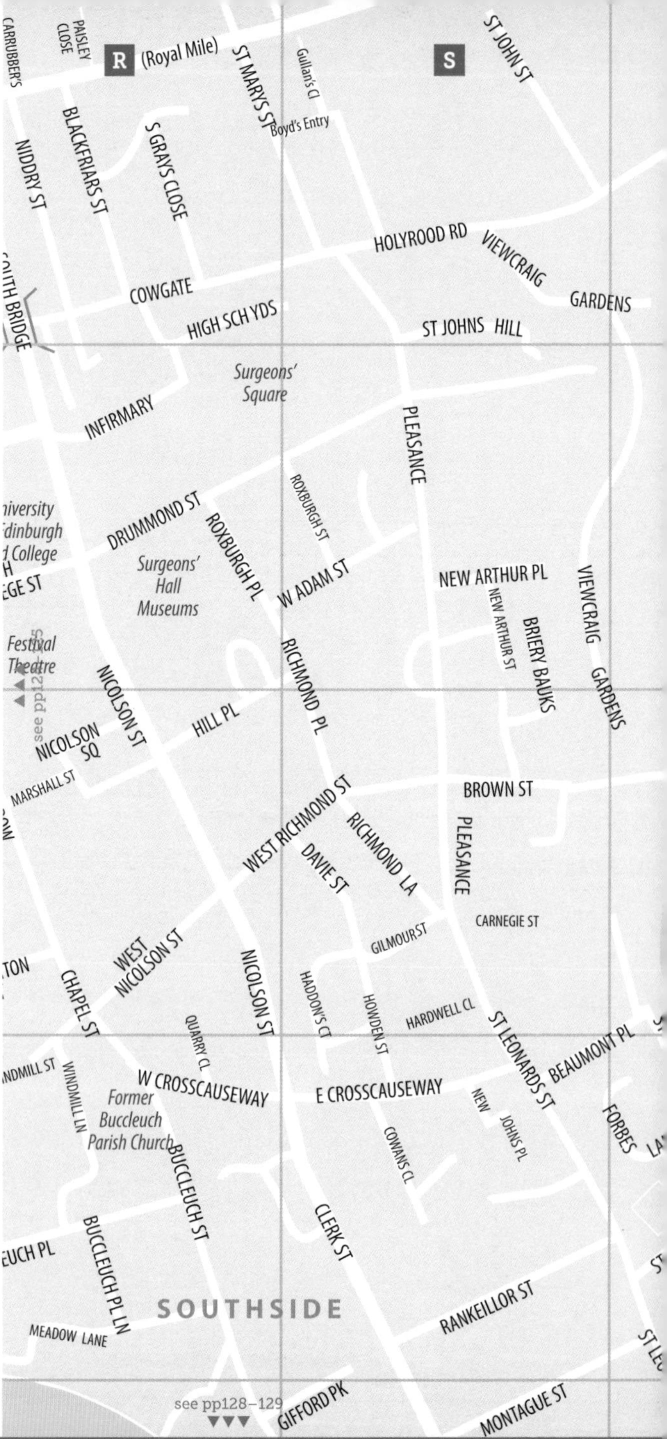

13

14

15

16

ROOD GAIT

QUEENS DRIVE

QUEENS DRIVE

ST LEONARDS BANK

ST LEONARDS

KSIDE ST

see pp128–129
▼▼▼

RD

Holyrood Park

Salisbury Crags

0   200m

0   1/4 mile

400m

▲▲▲
see pp120–121

WALKING TOURS

Some of the tour companies also offer customized and/or private tours.

Auld Reekie Tours
www.auldreekietours.com
Tours include: The Original Underground Tour, Ghost and Torture Tour, Terror Tour

The Cadies and Witchery Tours
www.witcherytours.com
Tours include: The Murder and Mystery Tour, The Ghosts and Gore Tour

Context Travel
www.contexttravel.com/city/edinburgh
Tours include: Introduction to Edinburgh, History of Medicine, Old Town Edinburgh, Worship and Religion

Eat Walk Edinburgh
www.eatwalkedinburgh.co.uk/index.html
Tour for Foodies

Edinburgh Literary Tours
www.edinburghbookloverstour.com/pubcrawl.htm
Tours include: Book Lovers' Tour, Literary Pub Crawl

Edinburgh Tour Guides
www.edinburghtourguides.com
Tours include: Royal Mile, Old and New Town, Leith Walking Tour, The Castle, Highlights of Old Edinburgh, School Groups, Robert Burns

Greenyonder Tours
www.greenyondertours.com
Tours include: Hidden Gardens of the Royal Mile, The New Town and its Gardens, Healing Herbs in the City, Patrick Geddes Garden Tour

Mercat Tours
www.mercattours.com
Tours include: Ghosts and Ghouls, Secrets of the Royal Mile, Hidden and Haunted, Historic Vaults, Ghostly Underground, Gallows to Graveyards, Paranormal Underground, Sin in the City, Misterios de Ultratumba (in Spanish), Tour and Tasting, Till Death Us Do Part, Schools, The Hellfire Club, Hidden and Hunted Treasure Hunt, Ghostbusting Birthdays, Murder Most Royal, Hidden Georgian Gems, Descend and Discover

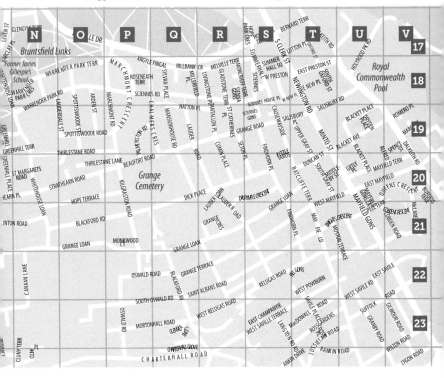

OOR Tours
www.oortours.com/
Musical Tour of the Royal Mile

The Potter Trail
pottertrail.com/
Harry Potter Tour

Real Tours Edinburgh
www.realtoursedinburgh.com/
Tours include: Free Tour, Literary Tour, Real Ghost Tour

Rebus Tours
www.rebustours.com
Tours include: Hidden Edinburgh, Walking with Scientists, McGonagall's Feat

Roam Edinburgh
www.roamedinburgh.com/RoamEdinburgh.com/Roam-Edinburgh-GPS-walking-tours-in-Edinburgh._Be-your-own-walking-tour-guide..html Hand-held guide, with selection of twelve tours using GPS

Sandeman's New Europe Edinburgh
www.newedinburghtours.com
Tours include: Free Tour, Ghost Tour, New Edinburgh Pub Crawl, Edinburgh New Town and Scottish Enlightenment, Mysteries of Rosslyn Chapel, Whisky and Haggis Tour

Saints and Sinners Tours
www.edinburghsaintsandsinners.co.uk/
Tours include: Old and New Town Tour, Castle Plus, Dean Village Tour, Graveyard Murder and Mystery Tour, Tour Français (in French), Royal Mile Tour, DCC Skinner Tour

Uncle Bob's Walking Tours
www.edinburghtour.com/uncle-bob-s-walking-tours.html
Tours can be downloaded to your MP3 player: Leith, Old Town, New Town, Pubs of the Old Town, Pubs of the New Town

EDINBURGH'S BUILDINGS, STREETS AND INSTITUTIONS

Please be aware that institutions change their addresses and correspondingly, buildings change use. Institutions may have also changed their name. In this guidebook, the name and address are given for the era in question.

Edinburgh can also cause confusion when a street changes its name. Here the former and current names are given, but sometimes a street still has more than one name along its length, or even from one side to the other. See in particular the Royal Mile.

Close is a courtyard or an entry to a courtyard. Many are accessed from the Royal Mile, but they may also have other points of entry. Some are not continuous, with the name of the close remaining the same on the other side of a main road.

High School of Edinburgh, also called the **Royal High School**. From 1578 until 1777 it was at the Blackfriars Monastery. A new building was erected on the same site in what is now High School Yards *Map p126* **S14** (EH1 1LZ), in 1777. In 1829 the school moved to another new building at 5-7 Regent Road *Map p118* **T11** (Old Royal High School, EH1 3DG). The High School Yards building became the Surgical Hospital in 1832 in which the University of Edinburgh held its anatomy classes, and was then acquired by the university in 1906. It now houses their Archaeology Department.

Hospital can mean a charitable school.

Land is a tall, narrow building.

Links are a golf course or land associated with golf, often at the coast.

Loan is a lane.

Luckenbooths

Meaning locked booths, they were permanent shops with shutters in the middle of the Royal Mile, running the length of St Giles Cathedral *Map p124* **Q13** (EH1 1RE). The timber-fronted buildings were between four and six storeys high and were erected about 1460 and demolished in 1817.

Medical School and medical instruction

The Medical School of the University of Edinburgh was originally at the Old College *Map p126* **R14** (EH8 9YL). It moved to what is now called the Old Medical School in Teviot Place *Map p124* **Q15** (EH8 9AG) in the 1880s. Freelance or extra-mural instructors in medicine and related studied such as anatomy operated from nearby premises in Surgeons' Square at High School Yards *Map p126* **R14** (EH1 1LZ). They competed for business by advertising, with those who could provide extras such as fresh bodies for dissection having an advantage.

Mercat Cross

Meaning merchants' cross, the most important one in Edinburgh was in the middle of the Royal Mile between the City Chambers and the current cross. The spot is marked with a large octagon in the paving *Map p124* **Q13** (EH1 1YJ). A place for public sale and bargaining, it was also where Bonnie Prince Charlie proclaimed himself Prince Regent.

Plaques are not standardized. A building may have one of numerous types or an inscription may be carved in stone. Often these are at first-floor (North American second-floor) level, so they may not be at first noticeable.

Royal Infirmary

After small beginnings in 1729 with six beds *Map p126* **R14** (plaque at the south-east corner of Infirmary Street and South Bridge, EH1 1YS), a hospital building was completed in 1742 at Infirmary Street. It is now the School of GeoSciences of the University of Edinburgh in Drummond Street *Map p126* **R14** (EH8 9XP), entrance now from the back of the original building. The Surgical Hospital was in High School Yards. The hospital moved in 1879 to a new building in Lauriston Place *Map p124* **P15** (EH3 9AU). It was sold and the hospital moved in 2003 to Little France (off map, EH16 4SA).

Royal Mile

Confusingly the Royal Mile goes by different names along its length. From the west, near the castle, parts of it are called Castlehill, Lawnmarket, High Street and Canongate, the last near the Palace of Holyroodhouse. Addresses for closes may be the High Street or Canongate as well as the name of the close. Lawnmarket is thought to mean either land market or linen market.

The Royal Sanctuary of Holyrood

At a time when being in debt was a crime, some debtors would take refuge in the Royal Sanctuary, which included all of Holyrood Park and some neighbouring areas. They lived in decrepit buildings near the Palace of Holyroodhouse, with the only surviving ones at Abbey Strand *Map p118* **V12** (EH8 8DX). The 'Abbey lairds' could leave for twenty-four hours from midnight on Saturday without fear of prosecution.

University of Edinburgh

The tounis colledge (the town's college) was founded in 1583 at the site of what is now called the Old College, then called Kirk o' Fields. It was approached up from the Cowgate on the steep Wynd of the Blessed-Virgin-in-the-Fields, then called College Wynd, now Guthrie Street. In 1789 building of the Old College *Map p126* **R14** (EH8 9YL) was started on the same site. It took forty years to complete and is still in use. Most of the university's buildings are now centred around George Square and its environs, with others at King's Buildings (off map, EH9 3JJ) and several other locations.

Wynd is a narrow lane.

Places of Note and Celebrities Associated With Them

Canongate Kirkyard *Map p118* **T12**
153 Canongate, Royal Mile, EH8 8BN
Closes at dusk

Clarinda *p22*
Robert Fergusson *p44*
James McLevy *p109*
Adam Smith *p74*

Church of St John the Evangelist *Map p124* **M13**
Cemetery entrance behind church off Princes
Street near Lothian Road, first enclosure on
right, sometimes locked, EH2 4BJ
Closes at dusk

Sir Henry Raeburn *p20*

City Art Centre *Map p122* **Q12**
2 Market Street, EH1 1DE
Free admission; viewing of collection by
appointment, ring 0131 259 3993

Francis Cadell *p12*
Hill and Adamson *p14*

City Chambers *Map p124* **Q13**
City of Edinburgh Council
Royal Mile, High Street, EH1 1YJ
Admission to entrance area

Peter Higgs *p62*
Hugh Miller *p71*
Sir Malcolm Rifkind *p93*

Dean Bridge *Map p120* **K11**
Queensferry Road, EH4 3AS

Ian Rankin *p50*
Thomas Telford *p94*

Dean Cemetery *Map p120* **I11**
63 Dean Path, EH4 3AT
Closes at dusk

Robert Adamson (see Hill and Adamson *p14*)
Dr Joseph Bell *p58*
Francis Cadell *p12*
Dr Elsie Inglis *p65*
Sir Henry Littlejohn *p69*
William Playfair *p19*

Dean Gallery
(see Modern Two)

Edinburgh Academy *Map p116* **M8**
42 Henderson Row, EH3 5BL
No admittance

Magnus Magnusson *p30*
James Clerk Maxwell *p70*
Muriel Spark *p53*
Sir Walter Scott *p52*

Edinburgh Castle *Map p124* **O13**
Castlehill, EH1 2NG
Admission charge

Henry Stewart, Lord Darnley *p101*
Greyfriars Bobby *p106*
James VI and I *p84*
Queen Margaret *p89*
Mary Queen of Scots *p90*

Edinburgh College of Art *Map p124* **O15**
74 Lauriston Place, EH3 9DF
Admittance by appointment

John Bellany *p10*
Dame Elizabeth Blackadder *p11*
Sir Sean Connery *p26*
Richard Demarco *p79*
Dorothy Dunnett *p43*
Sir Eduardo Paolozzi *p17*
Anne Redpath *p21*
Roy Williamson *p35*

Edinburgh University
(see University of Edinburgh)

Edinburgh Zoo *Off map*
134 Corstorphine Road, EH12 6TS
Admission charge

Sir Patrick Geddes *p61*
Chrystal Macmillan *p88*

Festival Theatre *(formerly Empire Theatre
and Empire Palace Theatre)* *Map p126* **R14**
13–29 Nicolson Street, EH8 9FT
Free admission, except for performances

Sir Harry Lauder *p29*
Moira Shearer *p32*

Fleshmarket Close Map p124 **Q13**
199 High Street, off the Royal Mile, east of
City Chambers, EH1 1QA

Deacon Brodie *p98*
James McLevy *p109*
Ian Rankin *p50*

George Heriot's School *(formerly Heriot's
Hospital)* Map p124 **P15**
Lauriston Place, EH3 9EQ
No admittance

Joseph Black *p59*
Greyfriars Bobby *p106*
Sir Henry Raeburn *p20*
Ken Stott *p34*

George Watson's College Map p128 **J22**
22 Colinton Road, EH10 5EG
No admittance

Gavin Hastings *p81*
Sir Chris Hoy *p83*
Sir Malcolm Rifkind *p93*

Grange Cemetery Map p128 **P20**
60a Grange Road, EH9 1TT
Closes at dusk

Helen Bannerman *p38*
Hugh Miller *p71*

Greyfriars Kirkyard Map p124 **P14**
1 Greyfriars Place, EH1 2QQ
Closes at dusk

Robert Adam *p9*
Joseph Black *p59*
James Craig *p13*
Greyfriars Bobby *p106*
James Hutton *p64*
John Kay *p15*
Allan Ramsay the Elder *p49*

High Court of Justiciary *(formerly Sheriff
Court)* Map p124 **P13**
Lawnmarket, Royal Mile, north-east corner
with Bank Street, EH1 2NT

David Hume *p63*
Dora Noyce *p111*

Holyrood Palace
(see Palace of Holyroodhouse)

Jack's Land Map p118 **S12**
now 229 Canongate, Royal Mile, opposite St
John's Street, EH8 8BJ

Bonnie Prince Charlie *p77*
David Hume *p63*

James Gillespie's School *(formerly James
Gillespie's High School for Girls)* Map p128 **N18**
22–32 Warrender Park Crescent, now
university student residences, EH9 1DY
No access

Ronnie Corbett *p27*
Dorothy Dunnett *p43*
Alastair Sim *p33*
Muriel Spark *p53*

James' Court Map p124 **P13**
493 Lawnmarket, Royal Mile, EH1 2PB
Access to courtyard

James Boswell *p39*
Richard Demarco *p79*
Sir Patrick Geddes *p61*
David Hume *p63*
Peter Williamson *p113*

Leith Hospital Map p118 **T2**
8–10 Mill Lane, now closed, EH6 6TJ

Dr Sophia Jex-Blake *p66*
William Merrilees *p110*

Lochside Walkway *Off map*
near Lochside Avenue, South Gyle, EH12 9DJ

Hamish Henderson *p82*
Norman MacCaig *p45*

Luckenbooths Map p124 **Q13**
since demolished, middle of the Royal Mile
near St Giles Cathedral, EH1 1RE

Allan Ramsay the Elder *p49*
Adam Smith *p74*
Peter Williamson *p113*

Mansfield Traquair Centre *Map p116* **Q8**
15 Mansfield Place, EH3 6BB
By appointment

Phoebe Traquair *p22*

Meadowbank Stadium *Map p118* **Y10**
139–143 London Road, EH7 6AE

Sir Chris Hoy *p83*
Yvonne Murray *p92*

Modern One *(formerly Scottish National
Gallery of Modern Art)* *Map p120* **H12**
75 Belford Road, EH4 3DR
Free admission

John Bellany *p10*
Dame Elizabeth Blackadder *p11*
Anne Redpath *p21*

Modern Two
(formerly Dean Gallery) *Map p120* **H12**
73 Belford Road, EH4 3DS
Free admission

Sir Eduardo Paolozzi *p17*

Museum of Edinburgh *Map p118* **T12**
Huntly House, 142 Canongate, Royal Mile,
EH8 8DD
Free admission

James Craig *p13*
Greyfriars Bobby *p106*
Douglas, Earl Haig *p80*
John Kay *p15*

National Museum of Scotland *Map p124* **Q14**
Chambers Street, EH1 1JF
Free admission

Robert Adam *p9*
Bay City Rollers *p25*
Alexander Graham Bell *p57*
Joseph Black *p59*
Deacon Brodie *p98*
Burke and Hare *p99*
Robert Burns *p40*
Bonnie Prince Charlie *p77*
Clarinda *p100*
James Craig *p13*
Dolly the sheep *p103*
Gavin Hastings *p81*
Hamish Henderson *p82*
Sir Chris Hoy *p83*
Sir Harry Lauder *p29*
Eric Liddell *p87*
Sir Compton Mackenzie *p47*
James Clerk Maxwell *p70*
Hugh Miller *p71*
Yvonne Murray *p92*
John Napier of Merchiston *p72*
Ian Rankin *p50*
J. K. Rowling *p51*
Sir Walter Scott *p52*
Moira Shearer *p32*
Robert Louis Stevenson *p54*
Thomas Telford *p94*
Phoebe Traquair *p22*
Irvine Welsh *p55*
Roy Williamson *p35*

National War Museum *Map p124* **N13**
Within precincts of Edinburgh Castle,
Castlehill, EH1 2NG
Admission charge

Francis Cadell *p12*
Hill and Adamson *p14*
Douglas, Earl Haig *p80*
Dr Elsie Inglis *p65*

New Calton Burial Ground *Map p118* **U11**
Regent Road, EH8 8DR
Closes at dusk

William Dick *p60*
Robert Louis Stevenson *p54*

Old Calton Burial Ground Map p118 **R11**
27 Waterloo Place, EH1 3BQ
Closes at dusk

David Hume *p63*
Peter Williamson *p113*

Old Royal High School
(at this site 1829–1968) Map p118 **T11**
5–7 Regent Road, EH1 3DG
No access

Alexander Graham Bell *p57*
Ronnie Corbett *p27*

Palace of Holyroodhouse Map p118 **V12**
Canongate, Royal Mile, EH8 8DX
Admission charge

Bonnie Prince Charlie *p77*
Henry Stewart, Lord Darnley *p101*
James VI and I *p84*
Mary Queen of Scots *p90*

Queen's Hall Map p128 **S17**
85–89 Clerk Street, EH8 9JG
Free admission, except for performances

Dick Gaughan *p28*

Royal High School, High School Yards
(at this site 1777–1829) Map p126 **S14**
now Archaeology Building,
University of Edinburgh, EH1 1LZ
Admittance to courtyard

Robert Adam *p9*
James Boswell *p39*

Royal Infirmary
(at this site 1742–1879) Map p126 **R14**
now School of GeoSciences, University of
Edinburgh, Drummond Street, north side,
EH8 9XP
No access

Dr Joseph Bell *p58*
James McLevy *p109*

Royal Infirmary
(at this site 1879–2003) Map p124 **P15**
now Quartermile, 1 Lauriston Place,
EH3 9AU

Prof Joseph Lister (Lord Lister) *p68*

Royal Lyceum Theatre Map p124 **M14**
Grindlay Street, EH3 9AX
Free admission, except for performances

Sir Compton Mackenzie *p47*
Moira Shearer *p32*

Royal Scottish Academy Map p122 **O12**
The Mound, EH2 2EL
Free admission for most exhibitions

Dame Elizabeth Blackadder *p11*
Dorothy Dunnett *p43*
William Playfair *p19*

St Cuthbert's Church Map p124 **M13**
5 Lothian Road, EH1 2EP

John Napier of Merchiston *p72*
Thomas de Quincey *p48*

St Giles Cathedral Map p124 **Q13**
Royal Mile, EH1 1RE
Free admission

Robert Fergusson *p44*
Sir Chris Hoy *p83*
Dr Elsie Inglis *p65*
James VI and I *p84*
Dr Sophia Jex-Blake *p66*
John Knox *p67*
Dr James Young Simpson *p73*
Robert Louis Stevenson *p54*

St Leonards Police Station *(Cygnet Theatre,
since demolished)* Map p126 **T16**
30 St Leonard's Street, EH8 9QW
No access except on business

Ronnie Corbett *p27*
Ian Rankin *p50*

Sandy Bell's Bar
(formerly Forrest Hill Bar) Map p124 **Q15**
25 Forrest Road, EH1 2QH

Aly Bain *p24*
Dick Gaughan *p28*
Hamish Henderson *p82*

The Scotsman Hotel
(formerly newspaper offices) Map p122 **Q12**
20 North Bridge, EH1 1TR

Magnus Magnusson *p30*
Lord Thomson of Fleet *p95*

Scottish National Gallery Map p122 **O12**
The Mound, EH2 2EL
Free admission

Sir Henry Raeburn *p20*
Phoebe Traquair *p22*

Scottish National Gallery of Modern Art
(see Modern One)

Scottish National Portrait Gallery Map p122 **P10**
1 Queen Street, EH2 1JD
Free admission

Robert Adam *p9*
Alexander Graham Bell *p57*
John Bellany *p10*
Joseph Black *p59*
James Boswell *p39*
Deacon Brodie *p98*
Burke and Hare *p99*
Robert Burns *p40*
Thomas Carlyle *p41*
Bonnie Prince Charlie *p77*
Henry Stewart, Lord Darnley *p101*
Dolly the sheep *p103*
Sir Patrick Geddes *p61*
Hill and Adamson *p14*
David Hume *p63*
James Hutton *p64*
Dr Elsie Inglis *p65*
James VI and I *p84*
John Kay *p15*
Alison Kinnaird *p16*
John Knox *p67*
Norman MacCaig *p45*
Alexander McCall Smith *p46*
Sir Compton Mackenzie *p47*
Queen Margaret *p89*
Mary Queen of Scots *p90*
James Clerk Maxwell *p70*
Hugh Miller *p71*
Yvonne Murray *p92*
Sir Henry Raeburn *p20*
Allan Ramsay the Elder *p49*
Sir Walter Scott *p52*
Adam Smith *p74*
Muriel Spark *p53*
Phoebe Traquair *p22*

Scottish Parliament Map p118 **U12**
Horse Wynd, EH99 1SP
Free admission to entrance area;
charge for tours

Aly Bain *p24*
Alison Kinnaird *p16*
Norman MacCaig *p45*
Ian Rankin *p50*

Surgeons' Hall Museum *Map p126* **R14**
18 Nicolson Street, EH8 9DW
Admission charge

Dr Joseph Bell *p58*
Burke and Hare *p99*
Sir Arthur Conan Doyle *p42*
John Knox *p67*
Prof Joseph Lister (Lord Lister) *p68*
Sir Henry Littlejohn *p69*
William Playfair *p19*
Dr James Young Simpson *p73*

Surgeons' Square *Map p126* **R14**
High School Yards, now part of University of
Edinburgh, bear right and through archway,
EH1 1LZ
Access to courtyard

Burke and Hare *p99*
Dr Elsie Inglis *p65*
Dr Sophia Jex-Blake *p66*
Dr Robert Knox *p108*
Prof Joseph Lister (Lord Lister) *p68*

Traverse Theatre *(formerly at West Bow, off Grassmarket)* *Map p124* **M14**
10 Cambridge Street, EH1 2ED
Free admission, except for performances

Kate Atkinson *p37*
Richard Demarco *p79*
Irvine Welsh *p55*

University of Edinburgh *Map p126* **R14**
Old College, South Bridge, EH8 9YL
Most of collection not on display, apart from
what is in the university offices; access to
quad and Talbot Rice Gallery

Robert Adam *p9*
James Miranda Barry *p97*
Alexander Graham Bell *p57*
Joseph Black *p59*
James Boswell *p39*
Burke and Hare *p99*
Henry Stewart, Lord Darnley *p101*
John Edmonstone *p105*
Dr Robert Knox *p108*
Eric Liddell *p87*
Sir Henry Littlejohn *p69*
Chrystal Macmillan *p88*
Magnus Magnusson *p30*
James Clerk Maxwell *p70*
William Playfair *p19*
Sir Malcolm Rifkind *p93*

University of Edinburgh *Map p124* **Q15**
Old Medical School and Anatomical Museum
Teviot Place, EH8 9AG
Access to courtyard; Anatomical Museum,
occasional open days

Sir Arthur Conan Doyle *p42*
William Burke (see Burke and Hare *p99*)
Dr Sophia Jex-Blake *p66*
Prof Joseph Lister (Lord Lister) *p68*
Dr James Young Simpson *p73*

University of Edinburgh *(formerly Moray House College of Education)* *Map p126* **S13**
St John Street, off Royal Mile, EH8 8AQ
Access to exterior areas

Hamish Henderson *p82*
Norman MacCaig *p45*

University of Edinburgh *Map p126* **R16**
George Square, EH8 9JX
Access to exterior areas

Thomas Carlyle *p41*
Hamish Henderson *p82*
Sir Chris Hoy *p83*
Eric Liddell *p87*
Norman MacCaig *p45*
Chrystal Macmillan *p88*

University of Edinburgh *Off map*
King's Buildings, Mayfield Road, EH9 3JZ

Peter Higgs *p62*
James Hutton *p64*
Chrystal Macmillan *p88*

Usher Hall *Map p124* **M14**
Lothian Road, EH1 2EA
Free admission, except for performances

Tony Blair *p76*
Sir Harry Lauder *p29*
Moira Shearer *p32*

Warriston Cemetery *Map p116* **O4**
42 Warriston Gardens, EH3 5NE
Closes at dusk

John Menzies *p91*
Dr James Young Simpson *p73*

Waverley Court *(City of Edinburgh Council Headquarters)* *Map p126* **R12**
East Market Street, EH8 8BG

Sir Patrick Geddes *p61*
Ken Stott *p34*

Waverley Station *Map p122* **Q12**
Waverley Bridge, EH1 1BB

John Menzies *p91*
William Merrilees *p110*

West Princes Street Gardens *Map p124* **N13**
EH2 2HG
Free access

Aly Bain *p24*
Allan Ramsay the Elder *p49*
Dr James Young Simpson *p73*
Robert Louis Stevenson *p54*

Writers' Museum and Makars' Court
Map p124 **P13**
Lady Stair's Close, Lawnmarket, off Royal Mile, EH1 2PA
Free admission

Robert Burns *p40*
Deacon Brodie *p98*
Clarinda *p100*
Dorothy Dunnett *p43*
Robert Fergusson *p44*
Sir Walter Scott *p52*
Robert Louis Stevenson *p54*

Glossary of Words Unfamiliar to Non-British People or Even Non-Scottish People

Advocate: A barrister, a type of lawyer who pleads cases in a court of law

Cooper: A person who makes or mends barrels

DIY: Do it yourself, one's own home repairs and improvements

Dustman: A refuse collector or garbage man

Football: Soccer

Hogmanay: New Year's Eve

Joiner: Carpenter, skilled woodworker

King's evidence: State's evidence, ie, giving evidence against former accomplices in order to get a lighter sentence or immunity from prosecution

Kirk: Church

Kirkyard: Cemetery

Local: The pub nearby to home or work

Lord Provost: Mayor

Makar: Poet or bard

Petrol station: Gas station

Sassenach: English person or Lowland Scot

Solicitor: A lawyer, one who doesn't usually appear in court

Twin set: Matching knitted tops, a cardigan worn over a sweater, now thought prim

Acknowledgements

Luckily for me, Edinburgh is a sort of village, where everyone knows everyone, so I was able to ask people I know for information. If they didn't have it themselves, they knew someone who might. Those who helped in this way, some providing photos as well, are Maureen Hodge, Arkady Hodge, Sandy Montgomery, Carola Small, Gavin Sprott, S R Halevy Spark, David Michie, Elizabeth Blackadder, Simon Coke, Anne Fine, Alan Mackaill, Mike Storie, Father Desmond Keegan, Ruth McIlroy, Tricia Staniforth, Muriel Morton, Marta McGlynn, Susan Bittker, Joseph Bonnar, Ruth Pelzer, Kate Henderson, Elizabeth Cumming, Mungo Dunnett, Richard Demarco and Terry Ann Newman at the Demarco European Art Foundation, Christopher Fryer, Calum McDonald, Chris Pearson, Rhona McLeod, Hugh Macmillan, Rebecca Ritchie, Vivienne Schuster, Kirsty Grierson, Neil Mackenzie and David Mach. I was also helped in a more official capacity by Aileen Stirling, Mortonhall Crematorium; Victoria-Rose Hodgson, Denise Brace, and Nico Tyack, Museum of Edinburgh; Joanna Soden, Royal Scottish Academy; Christopher Henry, Emma Black and Marianne Smith, Royal College of Surgeons of Edinburgh; Neil Fraser, the Royal Commission on the Ancient and Historical Monuments of Scotland; David Patterson, City Art Centre; Jill Forrest, University of Edinburgh; Karen Donaghy, Scottish Television; Edinburgh and Scottish Collection, Edinburgh Central Library; Scotland's People; Clare McCormack and Philip Hunt, National Galleries of Scotland; Katie Holyoak, Royal Collection Enterprises; Scott Irvine, John Menzies plc; the Library of Congress; the Wallace Collection; Caroline Milligan, the School of Scottish Studies; Gavin Browne, www.corries.com. Basic but vital help with photography was provided by Robert Young and Susanne Ramsenthaler. Essential moral support came from many, but especially Barry Winston, Maureen Hodge and Peggy Issenman. Special thanks go to them, and thank you as well to all who provided information, leads and photos, who listened and taught me so much about Edinburgh and its people.

Photo Credits

Many thanks to all who have generously supplied photographs or allowed them to be taken. Photographers who have kindly provided images are Doug Corrance, Colin Clark, Edinburgh City Council, Image Nation Photography, Marc Millar, Simon Hollington, Figos Photography, Alison Dunnett, Ian Mackenzie, Fiona Morgan, Graham Macindoe and Robert Rutherford at scottishfineprints.com and Jill Forrest. Photographs of John Bellany, the Bay City Rollers, Magnus Magnusson, Lord Thomson of Fleet, Dora Noyce, William Merrilees and Ludovic Kennedy are copyright the Scotsman Publications Ltd, Licensor www.scran.ac.uk. The photo of Alastair Sim is copyright Newsquest (Herald & Times) Licensor www. scran.ac.uk.

Photographs from Wiki Commons are the portrait of Alexander Graham Bell, Moffett Studio/Library and Archives Canada/C-017335 {{PD-1923}}; composite portrait of Hill and Adamson, George Eastman House {{PD-1923}}; portrait of Sophia Jex-Blake, Margaret Todd {{PD-1923}}; portrait of Robert Louis Stevenson, Ana Quiroga, alberto {{PD-1923}}; John Kay portraits of James Hutton and Adam Smith, Library of Congress {{PD-1923}}; portrait of Compton Mackenzie, Alvin Langdon Coburn {{PD-1923}}; engraving of Thomas de Quincey, Project Gutenberg, http://www.gutenberg. org/etext/16026 {{PD-Gutenberg}}; Crashandspin and YUL89YYZ; John Kay self-portrait, Walter Scott Library {{PD-1923}}; John Kay portrait of Lord Bannantyne, Harvard Library {{PD-1923}}; portrait of James Boswell, National Library of Medicine {{PD-1923}}; portrait of James Clerk Maxwell, engraving {{PD-1923}}; portrait of James Connolly, David Granville {{PD-1923}}; portrait of Earl Haig, Bain New Service, Library of Congress {{PD-1923}}; portrait of Thomas Telford, engraving 1838 {{PD-1923}}.

Photographs from Creative Commons are by Stuart Crawford at http://flickr.com/photos/potatojunkie/, William Melotti, Markus Grossmann, Kristin Dos Santos, Tim Duncan, Sjhill, Marius Kubik, Gert-Martin Greuel, LittleMissSilly, Grant Ritchie, Vclaw, Nick J Webb, Lokal Profil, Frederic Humber, Daffy123, Maltesedog, Robert D Ward; the photographs from Flickr are by peacay, camano10 at http://www.flickr.com/ photos/38045604@N00/, Ben Williams at bookslive. co.za, Mosman Library, Metro Centric and Daniel Ogren at http://www.flickr.com/photos/fast50.

Treboul Harbour by Anne Redpath is copyright the Royal Scottish Academy. *A Catte* is supplied by the Royal Collection Trust/ copyright HM Queen Elizabeth II 2012, www.royalcollection.org.uk. Other photos have been generously supplied by the Library and Archive, The Royal College of Surgeons of Edinburgh; the City Art Centre, Edinburgh; the Museum of Edinburgh; the Writers' Museum; the University of Edinburgh; David Michie; Carola Small; S R Halevy Spark; Kate Henderson; Stripe Communication; Tom Kitchin; John Menzies plc; David Mach; and Father Desmond Keegan.

The National Galleries of Scotland have kindly provided the following: from the Scottish National Portrait Gallery – portrait of Allan Ramsay by William Aikman; Robert Adam medallion by James Tassie; self-portrait of Francis Campbell Boileau Cadell (private collection); Thomas Carlyle photograph by Julia Margaret Cameron; Henry Stuart, Lord Darnley by unknown artist; Yvonne Murray collage by David Mach; Robert Burns by Alexander Nasmyth; Robert Fergusson by Alexander Runciman; Sir Walter Scott by Sir Henry Raeburn; and from the Scottish National Gallery – Sir Henry Raeburn self-portrait; *The Reverend Dr Robert Walker Skating on Duddingston Loch* by Sir Henry Raeburn; *The Progress of the Soul: The Victory* by Phoebe Traquair.

Edinburgh Museums and Galleries have helpfully provided or allowed the photography of the following: from the Writers' Museum – Robert Burns' cordial glass; lock of Robert Fergusson's hair; poem by Agnes McLehose (Clarinda); from the Museum of Edinburgh – Architect's Plan for New Town by James Craig; Greyfriars Bobby's collar; from the City Art Centre collection – Self-Portrait by Samuel Peploe; engraving of John Knox; photo portrait of Hugh Miller by Hill and Adamson; engravings of William Burke and William Hare. Other photographs and drawings are by the author.

COVER PHOTO CREDITS

Left to right, top row:
Sir Sean Connery, Stuart Crawford at http://flickr.com/photos/potatojunkie/
Greyfriar's Bobby, Joanne Soroka
Ronnie Corbett, William Melotti
J K Rowling, Daniel Ogren at http://www.flickr.com/photos/fast50
Ian Rankin, Tim Duncan
Madame Doubtfire, Doug Corrance
James Boswell, National Library of Medicine

Left to right, bottom row:
Lord Darnley, Scottish National Portrait Gallery, unknown artist
Sir Chris Hoy, Nick J Webb
Deacon Brodie, Edinburgh and Scottish Collection, Edinburgh Central Library
Mary Queen of Scots, Wallace Collection
Sir Harry Lauder, Library of Congress
Robert Burns, Scottish National Portrait Gallery, Alexander Nasmyth
Shirley Manson, Kristin Dos Santos

The information in this book has been carefully researched and checked, but we are only human. If you find something you think should be corrected, please bring it to the attention of the publishers, Crowood Press. We appreciate your help.

INDEX

Bold indicates one of the 100 Edinburgh celebrities and a **bold page number**, the page devoted to them.